Voters Expectation and Reasoning of Participation in Electoral Process

Field Assistants

1. M.A. Thirunavukkarasu
2. Mr. M. Gurusamy
3. Dr. S. Devaraj
4. Dr. Martin Taylor
5. Mr. Chellamuthu
6. Mr. K. Tamilarasan
7. Mr. Senthil
8. Mr. Kubendran
9. Mr. Sivakumar
10. Mr. V.S. Karthik
11. Ms. Subbulakshmi
12. Ms. Muthumeenakshi
13. Ms. G. Uma
14. Ms. J. Vanishree

Layout Design & Technical Assistant

S.P. Ramesh

About the Authors

Prof. Ganapathi Palanithurai, Coordinator in Rajiv Gandhi Chair, Gandhigram Rural Institute, presently heads the Department of Political Science and Development Administration, in Gandhigram Rural University, Tamil Nadu. He is also Associated with Centre Planning Commission, State Planning Commission of Tamil Nadu, Population Foundation of India, Ford Foundation, UNICEF, Rajiv Gandhi Foundation, CAPART, Ministry of Rural Areas and Employment and DANIDA (Danish-Indo Development Agency) in specific areas of activities in connection with empowerment of people. Prof. Palanithurai has to his credit twenty-nine books and seventy-five articles on three major areas, namely, legislative behaviour, ethnicity and Panchayati Raj system. He was recipient of Fellowship from Sastri Indo-Canadian Instituted, New Delhi and World Academy of Art and Science, USA. He is the Chairman of the Tamil Nadu Council for Sustainable Livelihoods. He was a visiting fellow in the MiGill University, Canada in 1989. He is a member of the expert committee constituted by the Government of Tamil Nadu to monitor the training programme for local body leaders.

Swati Sucharita Nanda has a doctorate in International Relations from Jawaharlal Nehru University, New Delhi. She is working in the development sector for the past four years. Earlier, she worked as a Programme Officer at the National Centre for Advocacy Studies, Pune. She is also a part of a project on the status of economic, social and cultural rights of the marginalized sections in three states in India.

Voters Expectation and Reasoning of Participation in Electoral Process

Editors
Dr. G. Palanithurai
Dr. Swati Sucharita Nanda

CONCEPT PUBLISHING COMPANY, NEW DELHI-110059

Cataloging in Publication Data—DK
Courtesy: D.K. Agencies (P) Ltd. <docinfo@dkagencies.com>

Voters expectation and reasoning of participation in electoral process / editors, G. Palanithurai, Swati Sucharita Nanda.
p. cm.
An analytical study of the 2006 general elections to the Tamil Nadu Legislative Assembly.
Includes bibliographical references (p.)
Includes index.
ISBN-13: 9788180694653
ISBN-10: 8180694658

1. Tamil Nadu (India). Legislature. Legislative Assembly—Elections, 2006. 2. Democracy—India—Tamil Nadu. 3. Political participation—India—Tamil Nadu. 4. Tamil Nadu (India)—Politics and government—21st century. I. Palanithurai, G. (Ganapathy), 1953- II. Nanda, Swati Sucharita.

DDC 324.095 482 22

ISBN : 13-978-81-8069-465-3
ISBN : 10-81-8069-465-8

First Published 2007

Published and Printed by
Ashok Kumar Mittal
Concept Publishing Company
A/15-16, Commercial Block, Mohan Garden
New Delhi-110059 (India)

Phones : 25351460, 25351794
Fax : 091-11-25357103
Email : publishing@conceptpub.com

To

THE DIVINE MOTHER

PREFACE

Citizens, who are concerned with democracy, look for a different course of action in our democracy to keep our democracy real and matured. When J.S. Mill made a statement that the representative democracy is the finest instrument for governance but to handle the fine instrument, society needs skill and maturity. Hence in the world only a few societies are having such a kind of character and maturity. But this lamentation was criticised. But now great realization has come among the scholars that the western pattern of representative democracy needs high level of understanding about the process of democracy for its success. Against this background, democracy in different forms suited to local socio-cultural conditions can be evolved and prototype model need not be followed as there is always a mismatch between the model and the reality of the society.

In India even after five decades of democratic governance, people believe that democracy is election. No doubt, election is the first step in democratic process and the way in which election is conducted will determine the quality of democracy. Democracy is a culture by itself. How the social, economic, cultural and political institutions conduct themselves in the larger political system decides the quality of democracy. In India, to conduct election in the political parties, the election commission had to exert pressure on the political parties. To make the political parties accountable, the election commission took several steps. Thus even our political parties are to be democratized. Our organizations and institutions have to be democratized. Our political parties have started practising any amount of foul means to come to power. In democracy, value adoption is more important.

Political parties have been enrolling huge number of bogus voters in the voters list and this has indeed, become a real challenge to the election commission. To lure the voters political parties and candidates have gifted the voters. Bureaucracy is divided and they also brand themselves as closer to political parties. Media in the market economy work in favour of their profit rather than giving the balanced views and news about events and issues. Thus the system is in deep malaise and this malaise has to be removed at the earliest otherwise people will lose hop in the parliamentary democracy. People have given perceptions and perspectives through their voting. Political parties and candidates have to learn lessons from the election.

Everybody was interested in knowing the results of the election. And this also includes us. But we are more interested and concerned about the people's thinking about the political activities of the political actors. What is their expectation from the government and how they look at the government and what type of bureaucracy they want are the real issues for the citizens who are concerned about representative democracy. Thus a survey was conducted during the time of election. To conduct the survey all my project staff helped me. The project staff from Rajiv Gandhi Chair, The Hunger Project, The World Bank Project spared their valuable time to interact with voters. I thank each one of them. Equally the respondents who spent their time with our staff without any expectation deserve appreciation. I express my deep sense of gratitude to them. The staff members of our department and members of my family deserve special appreciation as they do their work without encroaching upon my time and for which I express my heartfelt thanks to them.

G. Palanithurai

CONTENTS

Part – II

VOTERS' REASONING OF POLITICAL PARTICIPATION

LIST OF TABLES

LIST OF CHARTS

PART - I

EXPECTATIONS OF ELECTORATE

1 EXPECTATIONS OF ELECTORATE

Introduction

The results of the recently held election were obvious if one remembers the statewide study conducted and published by certain agencies, the results of which were spread through both the print and the visual media. Most debates and discussions held were on the forecast and queries concentrated on the methodological nuances. Political parties took cognizance of the newspaper predictions and acted upon them. Some of the parties, however, totally rejected such predictions. By and large the predictions have proved to be valid.

Election results communicate some messages and indications to the political parties and candidates about their participation. It informs the defeated party of the reasons for its loss. It also tells us about the reasons for which particular candidates are totally rejected by the voters. Factors are analyzed and decisions are taken at the levels of individuals and parties to gain in the next election. In the whole exercise, the process of election is being analyzed from the perspective of victory—victory for the individuals and the parties. Is this the right way to analyze the nature and quality of a democratic order? Quality of any democracy cannot be decided on the basis of victory of individuals or those of parties. But it is decided on the way in which the whole process is conducted. If fraudulent means are adopted during the electioneering process, it may lead to victory for the party, but it is a defeat for the people. People participate in the electoral process with certain assumptions and expectations. It is these assumptions and expectations that decide the course of political actions of the people including their voting behaviour and the choice of parties.

The 2006 general elections to the state legislative assembly is unique in many respects. Elections have their own arithmetic and chemistry. Arithmetic works on many of the occasions when the calculated predictions of the parties in the fray come true. At other times, chemistry works proving the victory of the charismatic leadership. This time both arithmetic and chemistry have worked together.

Electoral campaigns are unique, promises are unique, and election manifestoes are unique. In the same way, election results are also unique. Dominant opposition party is complacent in terms of its votes secured in the election but it is concerned with its defeat. The prominent ruling party is complacent with the number of seats secured but it is concerned with the poor vote share and minority status. Smaller parties are happy with the position of the ruling and opposition parties. This time, some of the smaller parties gained their strength and a few have lost their strength in terms of vote share. But the two dominant political parties have to necessarily rely on the smaller parties. For the political analysts, this election is unique as there is no violence in the election. Nor was there any major conflicts among the parties during the electioneering. Voting percentage has crossed 71. There was no rigging in the election. Though inferences are drawn from the election results, expectations of the people from the parties are not known explicitly. Hence, the need for the present study that was designed to look at the elections from the perspective of the people. This study is the logical sequence of an activity carried by us. At this stage, we consider it as a part of our efforts for voters' awareness.

Voters Awareness

Since its inception, the Rajiv Gandhi chair has been continually working towards building a progressive participatory political culture in the state of Tamil Nadu. During electioneering recently, it organized a three-day long voters' awareness campaign in Dindigul district prior to the Assembly Election 2006. The campaign focused on informing the voters of the significance of voting right, selection of right type of candidates and considering the background of the candidate for election. The campaign covered Nilakottai,

Athoor : Dindigul, Vedasandur and Ottanchatram constituencies of Dindigul district. The specific message given through the campaign to the people is as below :

- Voting is your right as well as responsibility.
- All who have names enlisted in the voters' list must vote.
- Voters must have general information about the candidate they are voting for.
- Taking money, gifts or help in terms of transportation for in return of votes is an offence.
- Alluring voters with money, gifts or transportation by the candidates is also an offence.
- The voters should have their voters' identity cards with them during polling.
- Voting in another's name is an offence.
- If anyone has voted in your name, you have the right to claim your vote.
- Vote for a righteous, disciplined and efficient candidate.
- If you do not prefer any candidate, you could register that under Election Rule 49 (o).

The political culture of a state in general and the electoral process in specific has been often questioned by the people. The main reasons of criticisms for both have been the effectiveness of the functioning of the political institutions, that is reflected through the manner in which they deliver both their material and non-material 'goods' and the manner in which the elites as well as the people relate to these institutions.

The term 'political culture' is being used in this paper to refer to the people's predominant beliefs, attitudes, values, ideals, sentiments, and evaluations about the political system of their country and the role of the self in that system. Specifically speaking, in the present study the phenomenon is being understood through the perception of the people of Tamil Nadu.

This particular study was done prior to the election 2006 with an aim to understand the manner in which the people of Tamil Nadu look at the present political culture of the state that has predominantly been determined by two political parties, DMK, AIADMK. What has resulted from this, is a sort of 'competitive populism' that could be best understood if one recalls the manner in which attempted to draw the attention of the voters.

Table 1.1 : Election Manifesto

DMK	*AIADMK*	*CONGRESS*
– Rice@ Rs.2a kg – Waiver of co-operative farm loans – free colour TV for poor – 3 lakh Government jobs – Rs.15,000 for girls' marriage	– 10 kg free rice – Waiver of co-operative loans – Free computer for students passing +2 – 5 lakh new jobs – 4 gm of gold thali for girls	– strong India and a prosperous Tamil Nadu – an efficient administration – employment opportunities through new industries – Stop commercialization of education – health care to the poor – establish a corporation for transportation of cargo and passengers in the eastern coast – Revival of the Legislative Council – Inclusion of Gandhian ideology in school and college textbooks – Modernisation of government libraries – A dole of Rs. 300 to handicapped with more than 50 per cent disability having an income of less than Rs. 6,000 per annum – Support for the growth and upliftment of workers engaged in khadi and cottage industries

(*Contd.*)

CPI	*MDMK*	*JANATA PARTY*
– Democracy, social justice, secularism affected during AIADMK rule	– reservation in educational institutions	– massive desalination along the coastline
– To take steps to free State's economy from World Bank's clutches	– diverting the westward flowing rivers to Tamilnadu	– solving water crisis
– To make efforts to make strike a fundamental right	– Tamil Ealam for Srilankan Tamils	– set up special education zones
– devolution of powers	– Tamil people, these pending projects should be immediately implemented.	– introduce three-language formula
– transfer of 50 per cent of the total tax collection by the Centre to the States	– Taking steps to safeguard the fishermen	– agriculture to be declared as an industry
– amendments to Article 356	– Without discriminating Tamilnadu implement the pending projects in Delhi	– introduce scientific support prices
– implement the Sarkaria panel recommendations		– introduce food stamps
– a balanced economic development of the State	– River linking	– temple management with autonomous bodies
– talks with neighbouring States to link the south-flowing rivers		
– Setting up a State Agricultural Commission		
– Establishing a national institute of bio-technology in the State		
– Curbing spread of genetically modified seeds		
– Extending the National Rural Employment Guarantee Scheme to all districts		
– Reviving the farm workers welfare board		

(*Contd.*)

CPI	*MDMK*	*JANATA PARTY*
– Distributing waste land to landless farm labourers – Eradicating all forms of discriminatory practices against Dalits – Redeeming Panchami lands – Safeguarding the interests of the Scheduled Tribes – Holding elections for Pappapatti and three other Panchayats reserved for Dalits – Protecting human rights and press freedom – Ending the 'kattapanchayat' system – Review of the Kachatheevu agreement		

The second reason for the present study was to look at the entire electoral process that is in general termed as political parties driven democracy where choice of the citizens is not reflected. Popular belief is that lack of interest as well as lack of awareness adds to this phenomenon. The space for citizens action has been reduced.

It must be made clear right at the beginning that the study in no way intended to anticipate the party (ies) that the voters were planning to vote. On the other hand, it was done with a clear focus to understand the entire gamut of issues that lie in the people's minds with regards to a progressive culture.

Statement of the Problem

Tamil Nadu has been celebrated by different agencies as a state to be looked up to as far as economic growth and human development is concerned. But not much discussion has focused on the nature of participation of the people in the political process from the point of view of enhancing a progressive political culture. The present study was done to understand the expectations with which people of Tamil Nadu participate in the political process and elect their representatives.

The study is intended to help the leaders and the administrators to understand the expectations of the people from them.

Methodology

The present study is based on a survey. The survey area includes both city and the villages in Dindigul district. It would also be pertinent to mention here that the survey in no way was taken up to be a serious academic research but was done to develop a general understanding of people's perception. Therefore, it was conducted in one village and one city which may otherwise not be considered to be sufficient enough for an in-depth academic analysis. The total number sample surveyed were 412 citizens which included men, women, people belonging to different communities and occupational groups.

In the heterogeneous random sample of 412 collected from the nearby (Dindigul) city and a village (Kalikampatti), the number

Chart 1.1 : Total Respondents

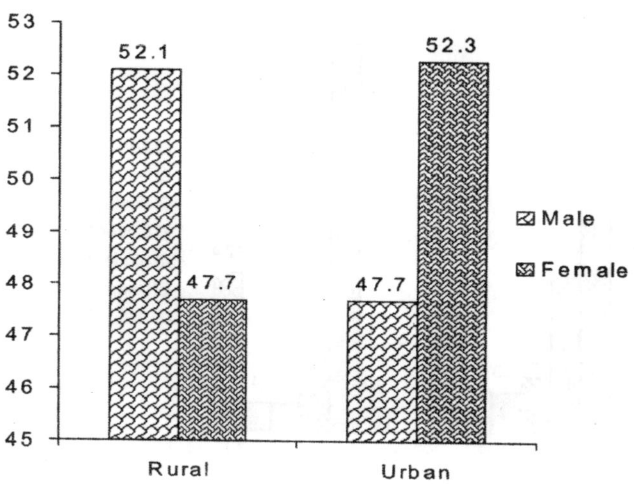

Chart 1.2 : Community-wise Respondents

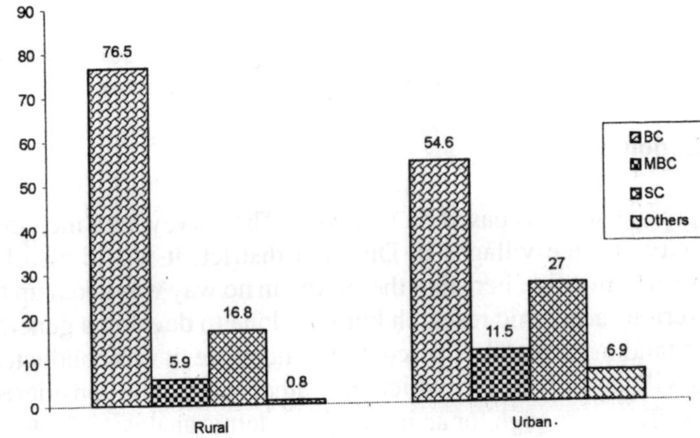

Chart 1.3 : Community-wise Respondents

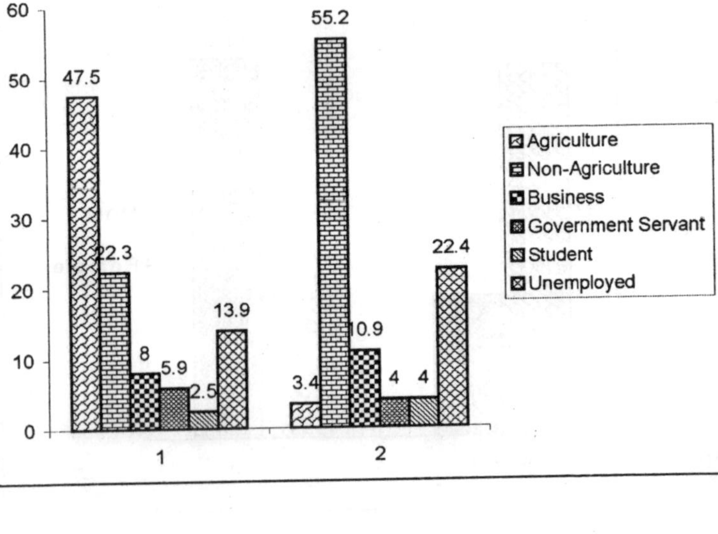

of respondents from the rural areas was 238 (57.8%) and those from the urban areas were 174 (42.2%). The charts below show the location/community/occupation-wise distribution of the respondents.

The survey schedule was designed to be an open-ended one to accommodate the fresh views of the people surveyed. Five questions mentioned below were asked to each respondent.

- What is the ideal government for the people of Tamil Nadu?
- What are the qualities of the ideal Chief Minister for Tamil Nadu?
- What should be the relationship between the ruling party and the opposition?
- What kind of bureaucrats do people of Tamil Nadu want?
- What services do the people want from the State?

Analysis of the Findings

The survey pointed towards the following as the most important issues for the people. The respondents stated that the most important qualities that they would ideally look for in their government, which included the chief minister, the opposition leaders and the bureaucrats are sensitivity and respect to people's issues.

People want their government to be receptive and friendly in its attitude towards them and more specifically, be pro-poor.

People's advice to the government

- People's perspective must be the first priority
- Stop partisan politics
- We need quality education and employment
- Fulfil basic amenities
- Be honest and transparent in all dealings
- Get the best from the centre for the state
- Maintain law and order effectively
- Better social security provisions
- Focus on the specific needs of the marginalized

The survey pointed towards some surprises. It clearly states that people of Tamil Nadu are tired of caste and communal politics and would rather have issues of raw development taking its place. These were answers that the researchers got not only from the upwardly mobile educated youth but the surprisingly from the rural folk as well. Development was translated into the availability of basic amenities at low cost or freely, creation of employment opportunities for the educated youth and vocational training for those not educated as well as developing infrastructures for better connectivity. An honest and transparent administration with no corruption, more accountability, timely work and a stronger role played by the institutions of governance is what the people demand.

What also came out of the interviews was a strong 'no' to any more feudalistic pattern, be it in bureaucracy or in the attitude of the politicians. It seems the days of *mai baap* are over and what is fast taking its place is a firm but not very clear idea of what can be called people's perspective.

What also became clear was the anger with the last government for not making use of its 13 ministers sitting in Delhi to bring about large-scale changes. No longer can Tamil Nadu's prosperity be seen as separate from that of India. For almost the last four decades, regional Dravidian parties have dominated the political landscape, keeping local issues such as caste identity at the centre of the debate. The cry among people is for a strong India and a prosperous Tamil Nadu.

(a) What is the ideal government for the people?

The answers to the open-ended questions focused on the need for better public relations from the side of the government. This is important given the fact that the leaders treat citizens of this country with respect only during elections and treated well by the administrators only when the leaders are around. No longer do people want this trend to continue. They want their government and their leaders to be honest, transparent and non-discriminatory in their dealings with the masses. People-friendly attitude of the government was considered to be the most important factor for 73.5 per cent respondents among the rural people and 37.1per cent among the urban people. Gender sensitivity figured as a very important indicator of a people-friendly government. What also got an important place in people's perception of a people-friendly government is its sensitivity for the poor and for those living in the interior parts of the state. While development-centricity clearly emerged as an important criterion for the people, more urban respondents (12.2%) than rural (9.7%) spoke about it. As expected, the rural respondents looked at development chiefly in terms of agriculture and felt that the demands of the farmers in relation to water scarcity, supply of power, availability of quality fertilizers and other needs must be sensitively handled by the government. It seems for the people of Tamil Nadu it will take a few more years and a few more promises by the leaders to forget issues like the suicide of the farmers in Karur.

Besides being development-oriented, the ideal government must take care of various segments of its population through creation of employment opportunities, looking after the people's basic needs and banning liquor. As the chart shows, 10.5 per cent of the rural respondents and 8.7 per cent of the total urban respondents would vote in a government that would provide employment to them. 10.1 per cent of the total rural respondents and 9.7 per cent of the total urban respondents would like to the government to focus on fulfilling the basic necessities of the people. 6.3 per cent of the rural respondents and 7.2 per cent of the urban respondents felt that the government should have a clear stand on issues such as banning the sale of liquor.

Table 1.2 : Type of Government.

What kind of government do you want?	*Rural*	*Urban*
• People-friendly	73.5%	37.1%
• Development-centric	9.7%	12.2%
• Providing Employment	10.5%	8.7%
• Basic necessities	10.1%	9.7%
• Abolition of sale of liquor	6.3%	7.2%

(b) Who is an ideal chief minister?

The respondents did have a clear idea of the personality that they want to lead them. The leader in their opinion must have a clear

Chart 1.4 : What kind of government do people want? Rural Respondents Opinion

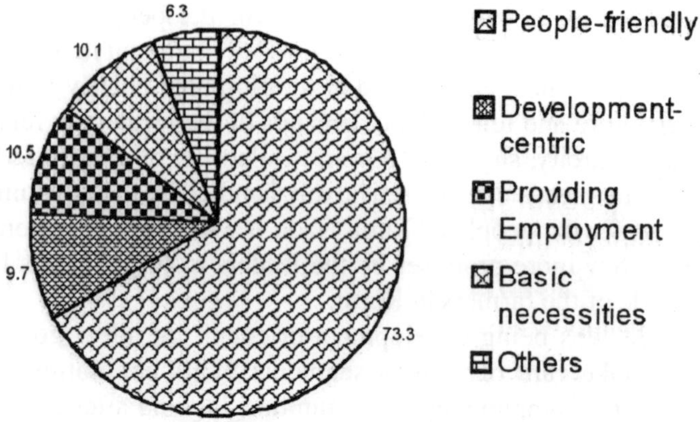

Chart 1.5 : What kind of government do people want? Urban Respondents Opinion

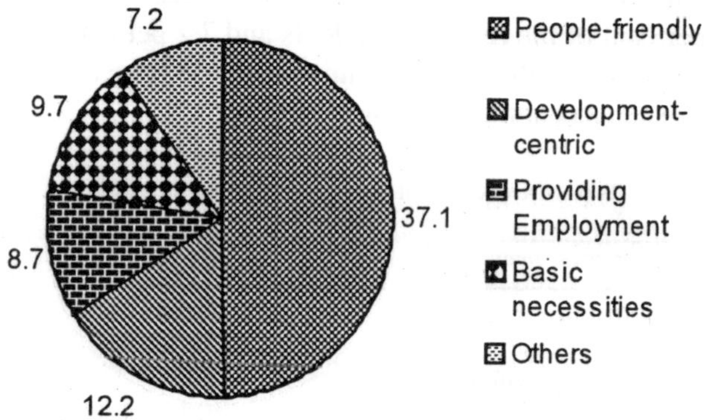

bias towards people in attitude. 88 per cent of the total urban respondents and 46.6 per cent of the rural respondents wanted a chief minister who relates to the people as a fellow citizen of Tamil

Nadu. 11.3 per cent of the respondents in rural areas 13.2 per cent in the urban areas wanted a clean, honest character to be given primacy in leader. 7.6 per cent of the rural respondents and the 21.8 per cent urban respondents felt that the leader should remember them after the elections.

While the survey did not consciously aim at making a conventional pre-election poll to know the parties coming to power, what became apparent during the interview sessions was the anti-incumbency factor lurking behind the answers. Majority rejected the autocratic attitude of the present CM, and justified the need for change on the ground. People did react trongly to the almost losing the opportunity to make use of the union ministers to bring about development in the state for which they blamed the confronatationist attitude of the CM. This factor was evident in the responses of 8.4 per cent of the rural and 25.3 per cent of the urban respondents. 21.8 per cent of the rural respondents and 23.6 per cent of the urban respondents clearly wanted their leader to take a strong stand against partisan politics played by the casteist and communal forces.

Table 1.3 : Kind of CM.

What kind of CM do you want?	*Rural*	*Urban*
• Strong in people's prespective	46.6%	88%
• Cordial relationship with the centre	8.4%	25.3%
• Respect promises made during elections	7.6%	21.8%
• Non-partisan to caste and communities	21.8%	23.6%
• Honest, not an opportunist	11.3%	13.2%

(c) *What should be the relationship between the ruling party and the opposition?*

Responses to the question on the relationship of the ruling with the opposition, what was evident was frustration with the manner both have been conducting themselves in public. 30.3 per cent of the rural respondents and 54.6 per cent of the total urban respondents clearly showed disinterest in being audience to the crude, theatrical fightings of the two. Support and mutual understanding over

Chart 1.6 : What qualities do people want in the CM? Rural Respondents Opinion

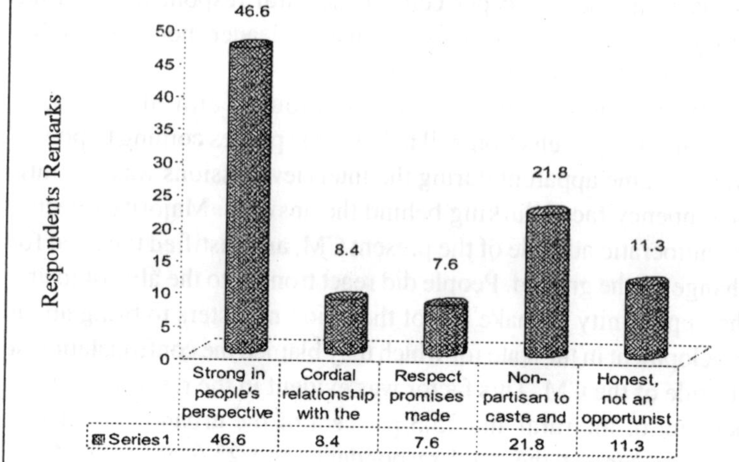

Chart 1.7 : What qualities do people want in the CM? Urban Respondents Opinion

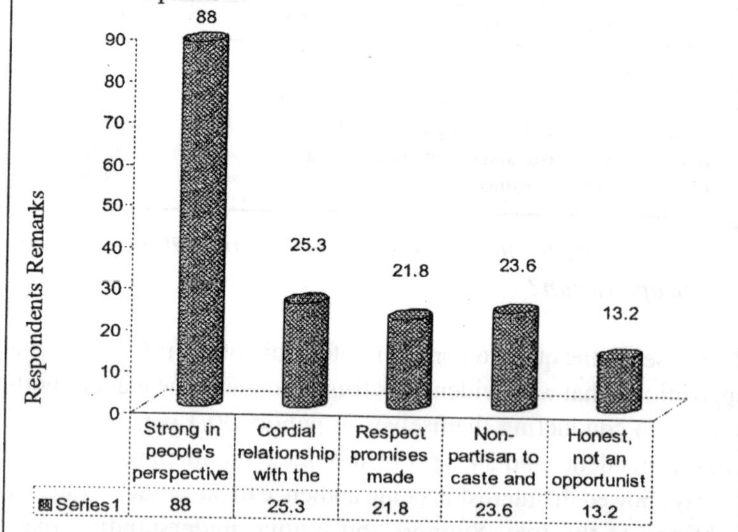

people's issue is something that 31.9 per cent of the rural and 85.1 per cent of the urban respondents wanted them to behave like. 20.2 per cent of the rural respondents and 10.9 per cent of the urban respondents felt that the opposition should make it a point to identify the mistakes of the ruling party, while the 5.9 per cent of the rural respondents and 9.8 per cent of the urban respondents felt that the ruling party must take upon itself the responsibility of resolving the deadlock, if any, between the two parties. The issue of distribution of tsunami relief kept coming during discussions.

Table 1.4 : Relationship between the Ruling and the Opposition.

What should be the relationship between the ruling and the opposition?	*Rural*	*Urban*
• End of the crude fighting era	30.3%	54.6%
• Support and mutual understanding	31.9%	85.1%
• Opposition should point out the mistakes of the ruling party	20.2%	10.9%
• Ruling party should take extra effort to resolve the deadlock	5.9%	9.8%

(d) What kind of bureaucrats do people want?

There is widespread awareness and condemnation among the respondents about masterly attitude of the bureaucrats. 25.6 per cent of the rural respondents and 70.7 per cent of the urban respondents wanted the bureaucrats to be people-centric in their approach. 39.1 per cent of respondents in the rural area and 51.7 per cent in the urban area wanted the bureaucrat to be honest and committed to the cause of social justice. A cooperative and service-oriented approach is what the administrators should adopt while dealing with the people, so said 11.3 per cent of the rural and 17.2 per cent of the urban respondents. The bureaucrats must complete all tasks on time and should not encourage redtapism is what 7.6 per cent of the rural respondents and 13.8 per cent of the urban respondents clearly stated. The administrators, especially the police must take seriously its role in maintaining law and order in the

Chart 1.8 : What should be the relationship between the ruling party and opposition? Rural Respondents Opinion

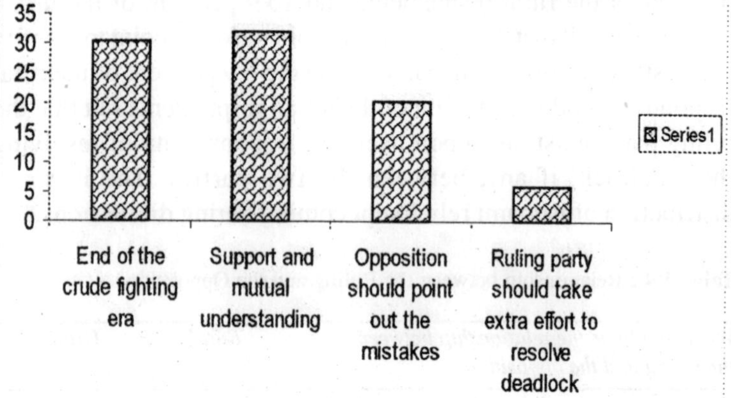

Chart 1.9 : What should be the relationship between the ruling party and opposition? Urban Respondents Opinion

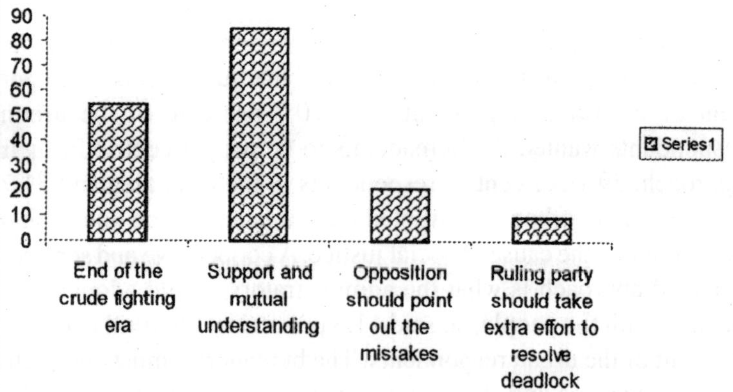

state, so felt 11.7 per cent of the rural and 16.7 per cent of the urban respondents.

Table 1.5 : Kind of Bureaucracy

What kind of bureaucracy do you want?	*Rural*	*Urban*
• People-centric approach	25.6%	70.7%
• Honest and committed to social justice	39.1%	51.7%
• Cooperative and helping attitude/service-oriented approach	11.3%	17.2%
• Timely do the work	7.6%	13.8%
• Maintenance of law and order	11.7%	16.7%

(e) *What services do the people want from the state?*

Among the services that people want the government to give primacy to are infrastructure, employment, water, health and food. 51.7 per cent of the rural respondents and 42.5 per cent of the urban respondents felt that infrastructure such as roads, transportation and communication needs to be given priority. 27.5 per cent of the total rural respondents and 69.5 per cent of the urban respondents spoke for the need to create more employment opportunities for the educated and skill-based vocational training for the uneducated. The public distribution system needs to be

Chart 1.10 : Kind of Bureaucracy-Rural Opinion

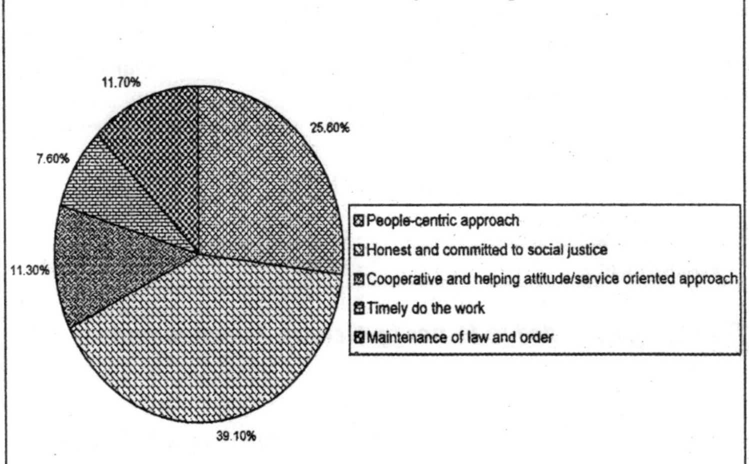

Chart 1.11 : Kind of Bureaucracy-Urban Opinion

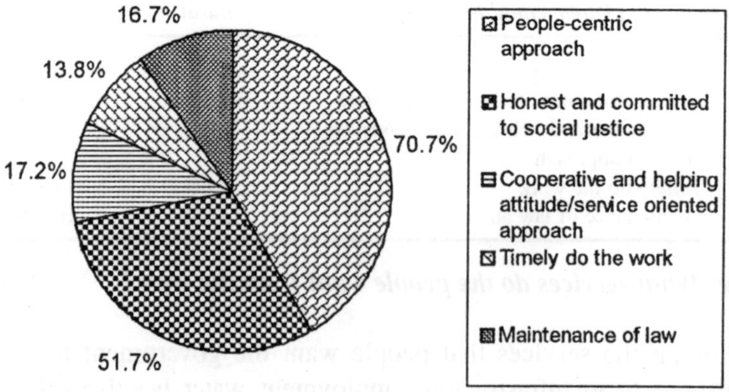

reinvigorated. So said 21 per cent of the rural respondents and 46.6 per cent of the urban respondents. Lack of availability of water is an issue for 23.5 per cent of the rural respondents and 37.4 per cent of the urban respondents. The government must take extra care of the health sector, felt 11.8 per cent of the rural respondents and 30.5 per cent of the urban respondents.

Table 1.6 : Services needed from the Government

What are services that should be provided by the Government?	*Rural*	*Urban*
• Water	23.5%	37.4%
• Health	11.8%	30.5%
• PDS availability	21.0%	46.6%
• Infrastructure	51.7%	42.5%
• Employment	27.3%	69.5%

(f) Priority accorded to Issues by Gender, Location and Community

A closer look at the manner in which different people belonging to different groups have responded to the questions reveals that the issue that got most number of votes was the lack of people-friendly

Chart 1.12 : What kind of service do you expect from the government? Rural Respondents Opinion

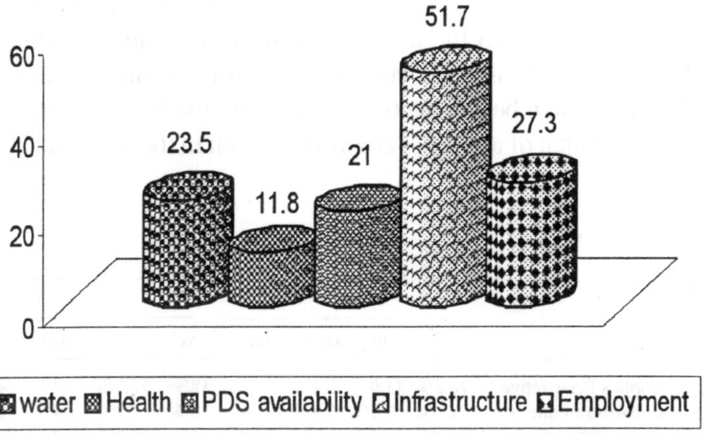

Chart 1-13 : What kind of service do you expect from the government ? Rural Respondents Opinion

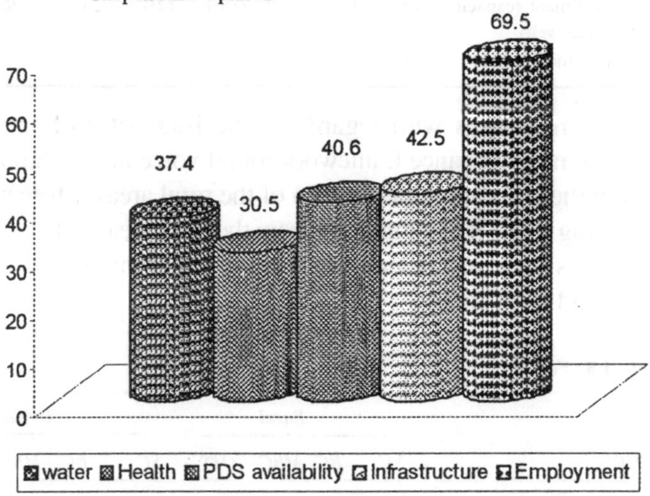

attitude of the government. The highest number of women for this category of responses were also found among the backward classes of the surveyed rural area at 46.5 per cent. Interestingly, more women (30.9%) belonging to the same community in the urban area also spoke about this issue more than other women in the same context. The responses of the BC women of rural areas stood higher compared to the men belonging to the same community (41.9%) as well as other communities in rural and urban areas. More rural men belonging to the BC community spoke about the issue than men of any other community both in the rural and urban areas.

Table 1.7 : Male.

AGE / ISSUE	*Rural*				*Urban*			
	SC	*BC*	*MBC*	*OTS*	*SC*	*BC*	*MBC*	*OTS*
1. People's Perspective	10.5%	41.9%	2.4%	—	18%	37.3%	8.4%	4.8%
2. No Partisan Politics	1.6%	7.2%	0.8%	—	6%	12%	2.4%	1.2%
3. Quality Education	2.4%	8.87%	0.8%	0.8%	6%	10.8%	2.4%	1.2%
4. Basic Amenities	8%	29.8%	1.6%	—	7.2%	14.4%	2.4%	3.6%
5. Honest and transparent administration	11.3%	49%	2.4%	0.8%	7.2%	14%	3.6%	2.4%
6. Employment (capacity-building, self-employment)	4.8%	23.4%	1.6%	0.8%	12%	24%	4.8%	2.4%

The responses with regards to the issue of an honest and transparent governance framework found voice mostly among the men in the BC community (49%) of the rural areas. More women belonging to the BC community from the rural areas (44.7%) spoke about this than any other women from the communities in both urban and rural areas.

Table 1.8 : Female

AGE/ ISSUE	*Rural*				*Urban*			
	SC	*BC*	*MBC*	*OTS*	*SC*	*BC*	*MBC*	*OTS*
1. People's Perspective	9.6%	46.5%	4.4%	0.8%	15.4%	30.9%	6.3%	2.7%
2. No Partisan Politics	2.6%	11.4%	0.8%	0.8%	5.4%	10.9%	1.8%	0.9%
3. Quality Education	5.3%	22.8%	2.6%	—	6.3%	12.7%	2.7%	1.8%
4. Basic Amenities	6.1%	29.8%	2.6%	0.8%	9.1%	33.6%	1.8%	—
5. Honest and transparent administration	8.7%	44.7%	4.4%	0.8%	8.2%	16.4%	3.6%	1.8%

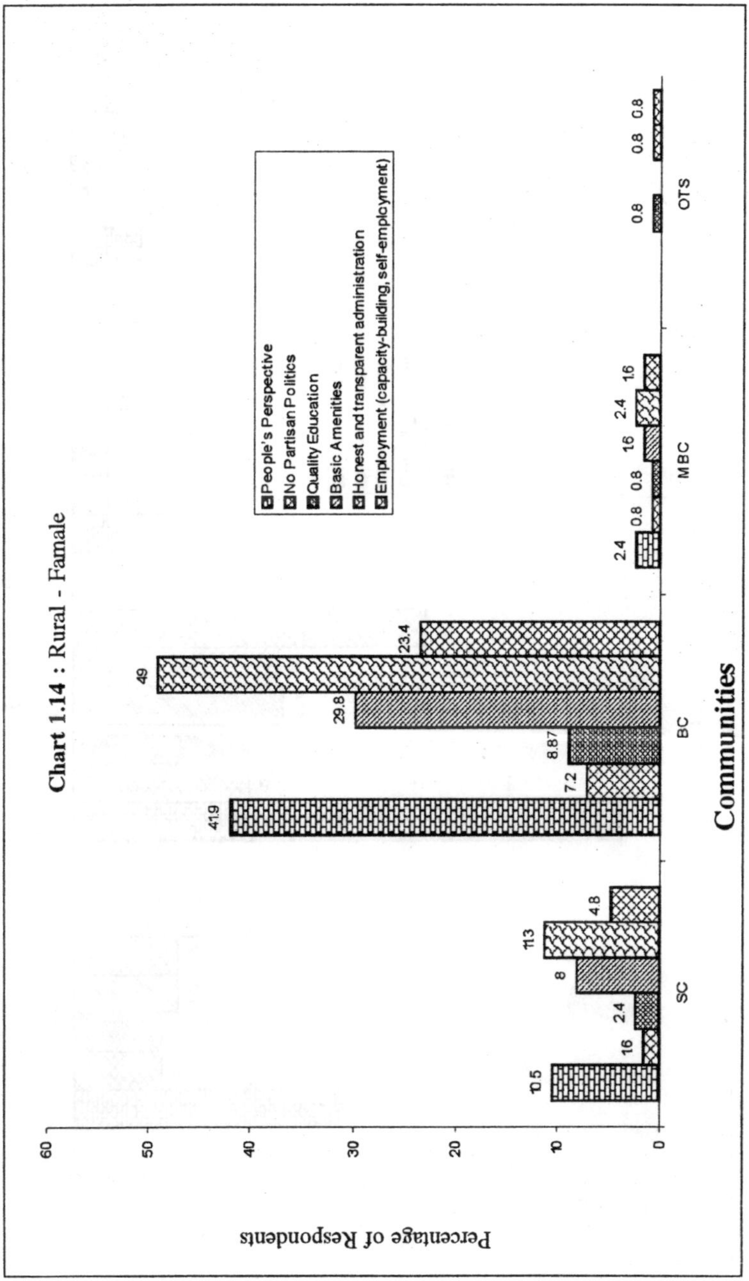

Chart 1.14 : Rural - Famale

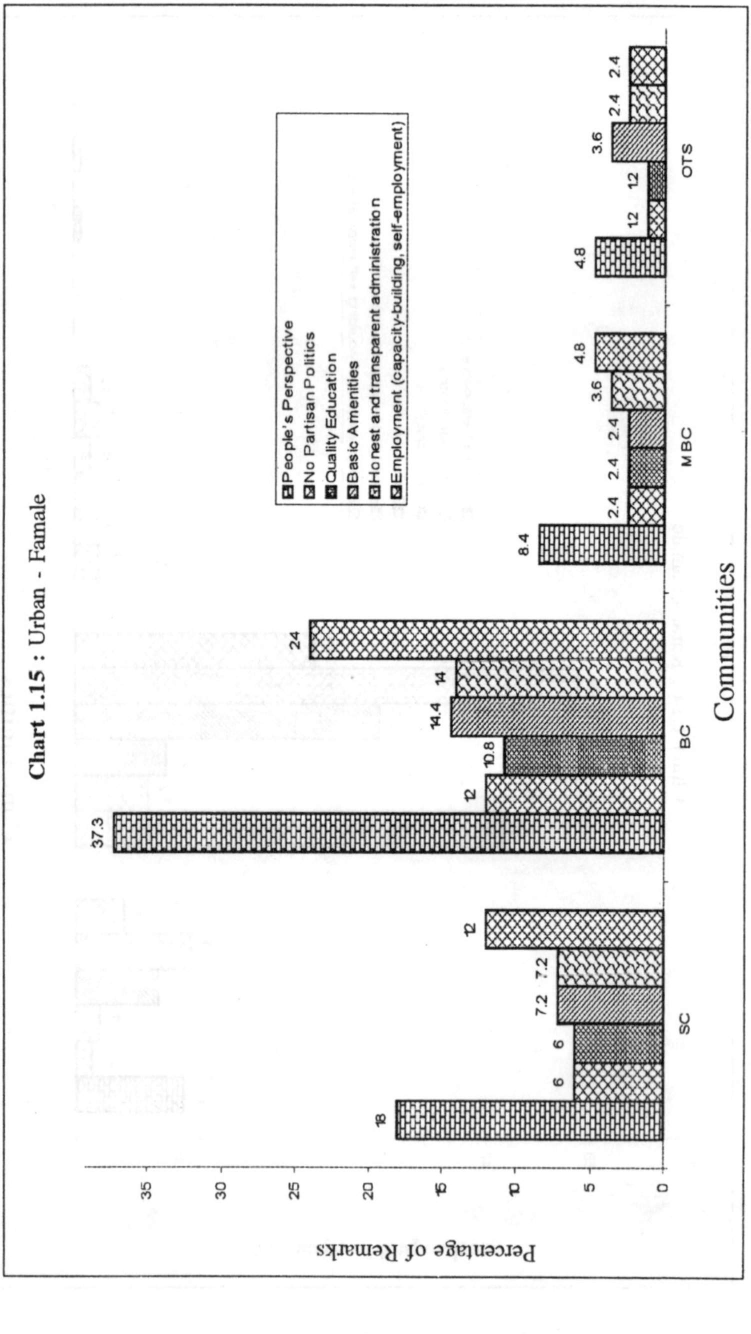

Chart 1.15 : Urban - Famale

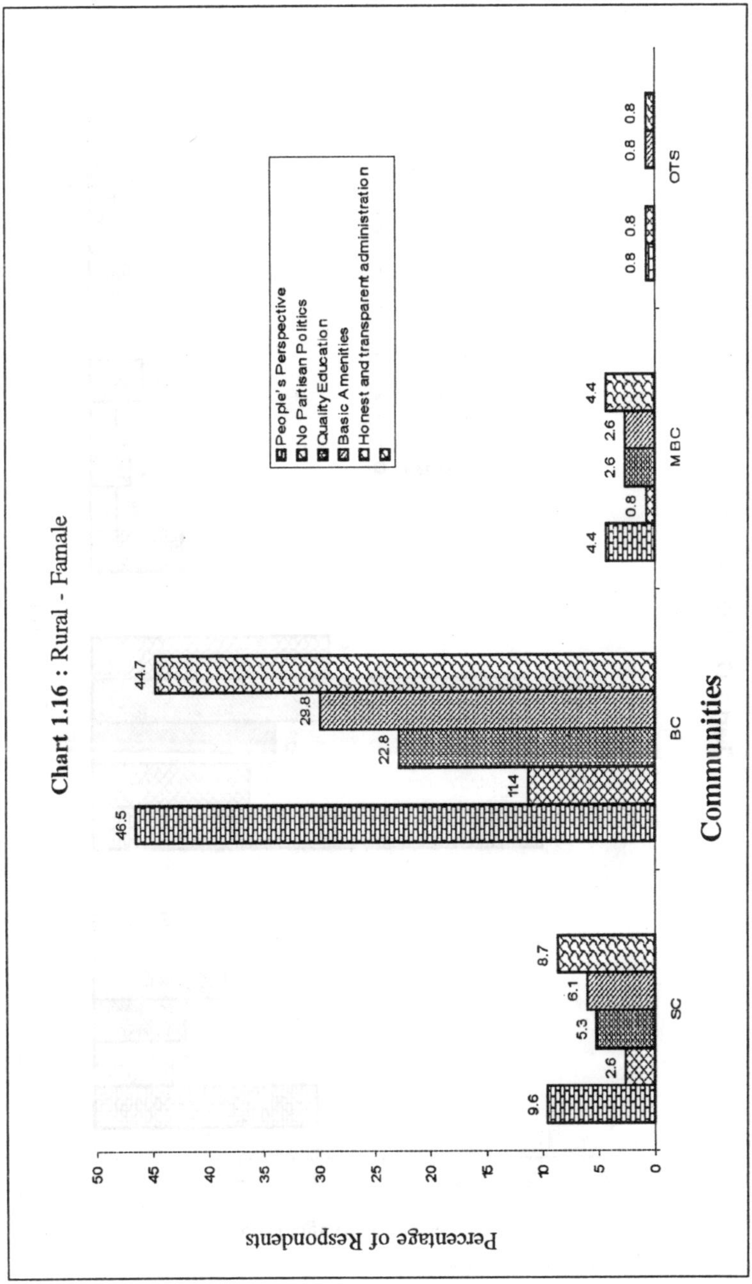

Chart 1.16 : Rural - Famale

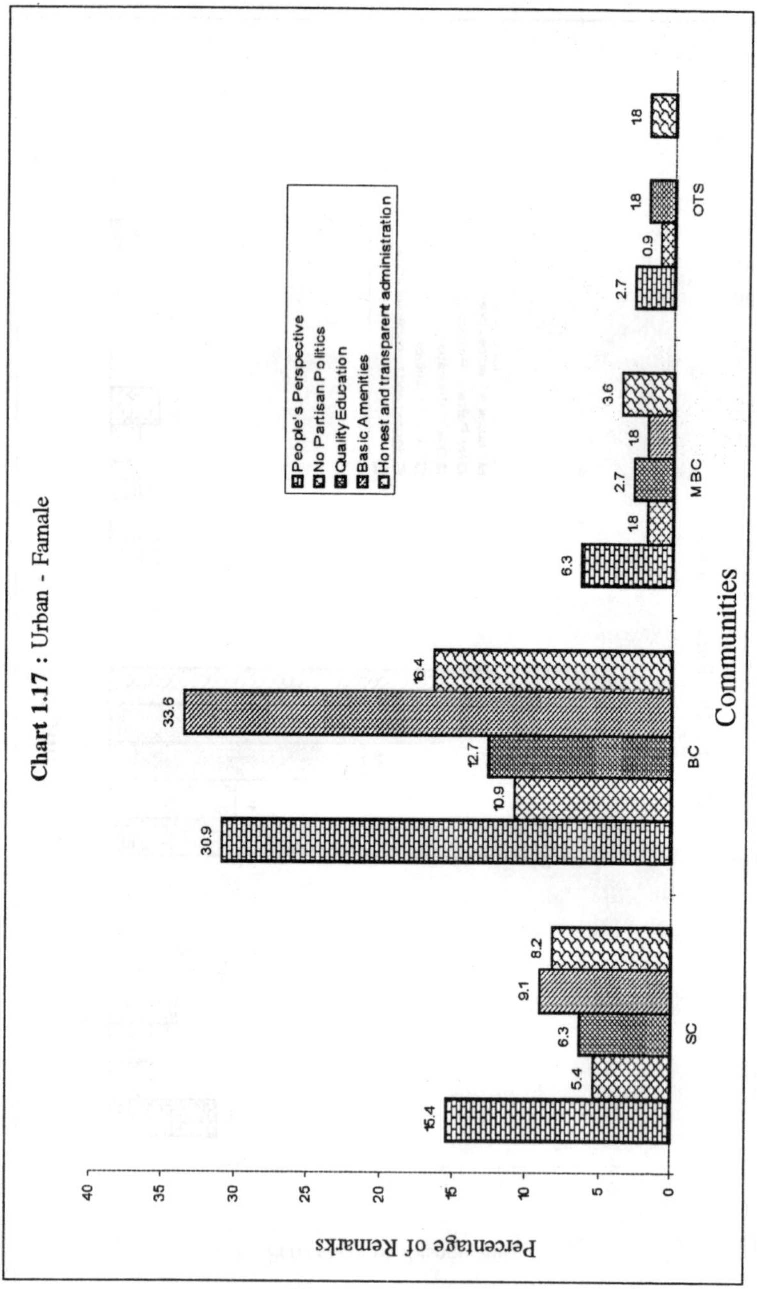

Chart 1.17 : Urban - Famale

The issue of quality education was taken up by more women from BC community in the rural areas (22.8%) than any other category. The BC men from the urban areas were the highest (10.8%) when compared to men from other communities both in the rural and urban areas.

The issue of basic amenities was taken up by 33.6 per cent of the urban BC women which is the highest compared to any other group of respondents. Among men, 29.8 per cent of the rural BC men fared the best with regards to this issue.

Employment as an important issue was taken up by 24 per cent of the urban BC men at the highest followed by 23.4 per cent BC men in rural areas compared to other communities. Among women, most responses were given by BC women (21%) of the rural areas followed by 20.9 per cent from the urban BC community.

On the issue of no more partisan politics, most responses (12%) were from the BC men in the urban areas compared to men of other communities. Among women, it is the 11.4 per cent was the highest number of responses that came from the rural BC community followed by 10.9 per cent from the BC community in the urban area.

(g) Major Observations

From the study, it is evident that the people of Tamil Nadu have a clear understanding of what the political system means and what should they expect from it. Both in the rural and urban area people. Both men and women, have strong political opinions. Then, the general notion that the voters are guided by the politicians does not stand to hold ground. But what must also be noted is that there clearly is a gap between the expectations of the people and the way 'political culture' of Tamil Nadu has been shaped. In other words, what is missing is lack of choice for the general public.

The study results point towards a strong desire toward among the voters to bring about a new political culture. The main components of this new culture as has been expressed by the people are:

- People-centricity.
- A broader non-partisan agenda to be followed by the parties.
- A more inclusive politics that does not look at the interest of the state separately from that of the centre.
- A political arrangement that is sensitive towards the specific needs of the marginalized and the weaker sections of the society.
- Honesty, transparency and accountability are the goals to be maintained as the core values of such a culture.

Among other points that emerge from the study is the fact that certain communities are more vocal than others. In this case, it was the Backward Classes (BC) community that very explicitly showed their awareness. What is also apparent is that the women of the BC community are as well-informed as the men from the same community.

People of Tamil Nadu have given a clear verdict. But it has been given with some hopes and expectations. At the most basic level, based on this study, these hopes of a people-centric politics, of progressing towards a responsible and accountable governance framework, and of justice to the marginalized. The new government has to bear the responsibility of this hope.

Annexure - I

People's Manifesto: Trichy

TIRUCHI : The "people's election manifesto," brought out by a group of voluntary organisations, has called for restructuring of the State finance policy so as to check the increasing imbalance between plan and non-plan expenditure, rising revenue and fiscal deficit.

Nearly 74 per cent of the State budget, the manifesto said, went to non-plan expenditure. Of the total plan expenditure, only 6.67 per cent was spent on shelter, 3.5 per cent for education and 2.51 per cent for health, it claimed. Over the past several years, revenue and fiscal deficit had also been rising. The State should come out with a transparent financial policy in consultation with public organisations. Fiscal and administrative changes should be made to ensure openness, transparency and participatory democracy should be the basis of the panchayati raj system in the State and gram sabhas should not remain mere platforms for receiving petitions. The State should also repeal Section 205 of the TN Panchayats Act, which empowers district collectors to remove panchayat presidents. A uniform TN Urban Local Bodies Act, applicable to all corporations, should be implemented. The rights of Dalits should be upheld by holding elections to the Keeripatti, Pappapatti, Nattarmangalam and Kottakachiyenandal panchayats, the manifesto said.

It also called for steps to protect the unorganised sector workers and low-income groups from the impact of globalisation. Common property resources and common village resources should be protected from privatisation.

The manifesto, brought out jointly by the Tamil Nadu Alliance for Right to Education and Equity (TAFRE), Campaign for Equity and Equality in Tsunami Rehabilitation (CEETR) and Child Rights and You (CRY), also discusses in detail various other issues, including the rights of the labour class, Dalits, women and children and puts forward various demands. The document was released here on Saturday by N. Radha, State Convener of the Campaign Against Child Labour. Social activist and organic farming votary G. Nammazhvar received the document.

The document also called for the establishment of a Software Park in Tiruchi district to tap the huge human resource potential of the district. The district has seen little industrial development over the past 25 years despite being a district with a good literacy ratio.

It also demanded steps to check the pollution of rivers and other water resources in the district. A new bridge should be constructed across the Coleroon river in the city to replace the existing old bridge.

Referring to the frequent flooding of the residential colonies in the city, it pleaded for urgent steps to remove encroachments on watercourses. The unplanned growth of the city should be checked and integrated bus stand established.

The document also discussed specific issues in each of the nine constituencies in the district and put forward several locale-specific demands.

Source : The Hindu, Sunday, April 30, 2006.

Annexure - II

People's Manifesto: Greater Chennai

CHENNAI: Reiterating that the demands of the city residents have been ignored in the manifestos of all political parties, greater Chennai Confederation, a newly formed association of various residents welfare associations in the city, on Tuesday released a "people's manifesto."

Burning of Garbage

Preservation of water bodies, a stern 'no' to the proposed airport expansion, prevention of dumping and burning of garbage at Kodungaiyur and Perungudi and a demand for more flyovers and bridges to decongest the city were given priority in the manifesto released at a meeting attended by more than 400 residents' welfare association members at a hotel in Koyambedu.

M.B. Nirmal, founder of Exnora International and convener of the Confederation, said the manifesto was not political in nature but merely a reflection of the true demands of the city residents.

The Confederation has suggested that the State Government must set up a "Water Body Conservation Board" to look after preservation and protection of water bodies.

Rampant Encroachments

"The rampant encroachments of waterways and lakes are proof that government agencies such as the Public Works Department and the police have failed miserably to protect them. So a separate government wing is necessary. Also the government should consider booking encroachers under the Goondas Act," speakers at the meeting said. They opposed the plans for expansion of the Meenambakkam airport, suggesting that a new airport could be set up outside the city. The manifesto read: "The world over airports are located outside major cities. We suggest that the airport could be built in Sriperumbudur and it could be connected by fast point-to-point train and two-tier road."

The residents' welfare association representatives also vouched for decentralised garbage management in the city and a comprehensive ban on the burning of waste.

Focal Point

Another focal point of the meeting was that North Chennai suffered neglect when compared with the rest of the city.

Speakers resolved to meet under the new Confederation regularly to highlight civic issues in the Greater Chennai region. Contact the Confederation by phone at 52193595 or 24759477.

Source : The Hindu, Thursday, April 20, 2006.

Annexure - III

Children's Manifesto: Coimbatore

COIMBATORE: Hundreds of children gathered at St. Francis Higher Secondary School on Tuesday. Cheering all along, they welcomed the candidates contesting the Assembly elections to their midst. Most of them did not even know what elections meant. But they knew one thing for sure—that many like them had lost their childhood to torture, abuse and beggary.

The children who assembled here to present a "children's manifesto" appealed to the candidates to help them get back the innocence of childhood.

Providing free and quality education from LKG to Plus-Two was their primary demand. Every village should provide facilities for education up to Plus-Two and children from shelter homes should be given special preference in educational and job opportunities, they said. They requested the Government to empower Non-Government Organisations (NGOs) working for children to rescue bonded child labourers. The right to enter the place of work and rescue child labourers is vested only with the Labour Department. If NGOs were also bestowed with the authority, the number of child workers could be brought down substantially, said Fr. John Dharman, Director of Don Bosco Anbu Illam.

Anbu Illam's Social Service Society and several other child rights organisations organised the event. Children from homes at Tirupur and Avanashi participated in the event. Individuals or institutions employing children below 18 years of age should be brought to book, they demanded. The manifesto sought assistance to build and maintain child help centres at Palladam, Avanashi,

Tirupur and Pollachi as a lot of children from these districts poured into Coimbatore city in search of labour.

The rest of the demands related to basic issues concerning children's rights such as violence, sexual abuse, trafficking and female infanticide. Torture or abuse of children and crimes against them should be prevented and the offenders should be punished, they said.

Coalition of Child Rights Networks of Tamil Nadu and Pondicherry drafted the manifesto when they organised a workshop for children in Chennai in February.

Nearly 100 children attended the two-day workshop, which helped them identify their needs and formulate them into demands. The manifesto also demanded clean classrooms and eating spaces in addition to free electricity and (Coimbatore East) were the candidates who attended the event. Water supply to their schools. Liquor shops near schools and playgrounds should be relocated, it said.

Former Minister Pongalur N. Palanisamy of the Dravida Munnetra Kazhagam (Coimbatore East Constituency), T. Malaravan, All India Anna Dravida Munnetra Kazhagam (Coimbatore West), A. Soundararajan, Communist Party of India (Marxist) (Singanallur), S.Maheshwari, Congress (Coimbatore West) and G. Mary, Desiya Murppokku Dravida Kazhagam.

Source : The Hindu, Wednesday, May 3, 2006.

Annexure - IV

Tamil Nadu Legislative Assembly Elections— 2006
DMK ELECTION MANIFESTO

Election Promises

We will do what we have said;
We will say what we have done!

Agricultural Development

- We will waive all the cooperative loans given to small and marginal farmers.
- In order to see that the farmers who cultivate paddy, sugarcane, cotton and chillies are not affected, subsidy and price support will be provided to them.
- Within three months after the sugarcane is procured by the cooperative public sector and private sugar mills, we will take steps to make full payment on the basis of the minimum support price fixed by the Central Government and the additional price given by the State Government.
- We will take steps to see that the lorry freight so far paid by the sugarcane farmers is borne by the management itself.
- We will take necessary steps to bring back the agricultural labourers who went to other states in search of livelihood and make them once again get involved in agricultural production.
- We will provide opportunities for the students in the agricultural families to pursue their education and also provide them scholarships. We will also provide

opportunities for the dropouts on account of the migration of their families to the other states to continue their education.

Free Electricity Scheme

- In addition to our promise that the DMK Government will continue the free electricity scheme, we assure that the scheme will be expanded to those who got electricity connection by paying special fees on a priority basis.
- At present, electricity connection is given for pumpsets which are beyond a distance of 200 metres from the river bed. We will reduce it to 100 metres.
- In order to provide incentive to agriculture, we will establish National Institute of Bio-Technology Wasteland Development.
- During the ADMK regime, though it announced that the wastelands owned by the Government would be given to landless agricultural labour, it had given away the lands to Indian and foreign firms. We will redeem them. A total of approximately 55 lakhs acres of wasteland will be distributed to poor agricultural families at the rate of 2 acres per family.
- We will find out ways and means of converting dry lands and wastelands into proper agricultural lands by making use of new technologies like Micro Watershed Management.
- We will provide incentives for cultivation of cashew in wastelands and introduce new varieties of cashew that increase the yield and make arrangements for increasing the exports.
- We will take serious steps to provide incentives for the cultivation of Jatropha, that will provide an alternative source of energy in future.
- In order to provide incentives for farmers cultivating sugarcane, we will take steps to make the sugar mills produce Ethanol.

- To provide opportunities for the children of agricultural workers in the southern districts to get employment and self-employment in agriculture, 40 boys and girls will be given all facilities to study degree course in agriculture in the Agricultural Research Stations in five southern districts.
- Steps will be taken to increase the height of the Mullaiperiyar Dam to 152 feet which is a longstanding demand of the farmers of the southern states. We will also recommend for the immediate implementation of Supreme Court order in this regard.
- We will set up Horticulture Marketing Structures to increase the export of horticultural produce like fruits and flowers and medicinal herbs and to sell the horticultural products.
- We will make efforts to set up Regional Horticultural Board in Tamil Nadu and National Institute of Plant Biology at the all-India level.
- We will insist the Central Government that farmers growing tea should get fair price for their produce.
- We will draw up schemes for the farmers growing coconuts to get a fair price and also for compensating those affected financially whenever coconuts were struck by disease.
- In addition to re-establishing Palm Workers Welfare Board, all steps will be taken for promoting their welfare is being done in the neighbouring States.
- We will draw up and implement schemes for production, preservation and export of processed food products on a commercial basis.
- We will expand the Micro Finance groups in all districts for increasing employment opportunities in village and cottage industries and for promoting self-employment opportunities.
- In the event of the natural death of farmers who have borrowed money from the cooperative banks, we will waive the entire principal amount and interest due to the cooperative banks.
- We will set up an Agricultural Development Council at the State level to examine the problems faced by the

agricultural sector including agricultural debt and to suggest immediate remedies to get a fair price for the produce of the farmers and to fix the minimum support price.

- We will implement comprehensive crop insurance scheme for all farmers.
- Besides improving water resources and implementing agricultural schemes, we will take steps for handing over irrigation sources to the farmers.
- As a continuation of the improvement scheme of Palar and Thamiraparani river beds implemented during the DMK rule under the Integrated Development Scheme, we will make efforts for the expansion of that scheme for other river beds.
- Besides making efforts for the linking of national rivers, as a first step, we will strive hard for linking the rivers in the South.
- We will implement the desilting of major and minor irrigation tanks on a continuous basis.
- We will evolve a special policy for cattle development and protection and implement new schemes. Besides, we will also achieve targets for production of milk and milk products which have not been reached so far.

Industries

- Development of large, small and tiny industries.
- In order to provide incentives for large, medium and small scale industries, cottage and tiny industries, we will adopt a new approach and with the help of Central Government departments and financial institutions, we will take steps to make Tamil Nadu attain industrial progress once again, increase employment opportunities and put it on the path of development.
- We will take a census of the raw materials available at the regional level and take steps for increasing the handicrafts products based on them. We will provide technical and

financial help for the centres meant for them and increase the employment opportunities in villages.

- To help the small traders become prosperous and to make them free from the clutches of usury (exhorbitant rates of interest) appropriate steps will be taken to provide weekly credit for them through cooperative banks on easy terms.
- Efforts will be made for the immediate implementation of Hi-Tech Park Scheme at Nanguneri, the work for which commenced during the DMK rule but discontinued later during the ADMK regime.

Education

- We will immediately fill all the vacancies of teachers in Primary and High Schools.
- We will pave the way for providing uniform standard of education of good quality for all people of Tamil Nadu.
- The scheme introduced in nurseries for teaching young children in the medium of mother tongue gradually, could not be implemented for reasons of the so-called rights of parents. Still efforts will be made to encourage them to learn through the medium of mother tongue in schools.
- We will find a suitable way for making all students in schools under different streams study Tamil language also as a subject.
- In all schools and in all class rooms, we will provide facilities for computer training.
- All the Guest Lecturers on consolidated pay in Government Arts colleges will be appointed on a permanent basis following the rule of Reservation. Apart from this, about 1700 vacancies of lecturers will be filled immediately.
- The present self-financing courses in Government colleges which provide opportunities only for those who can afford will be converted into general courses and fees will be fixed as in other courses.
- We will reduce the fees charged in the medical and

engineering courses and degree courses in colleges which have been increased ten times during the ADMK regime.

- We will translate into action our objective of one medical college in each district.
- We will take action to introduce teacher training courses (B.Ed and Diploma) in one Government college in every district.
- We will take appropriate steps to ensure that in the post-graduate course in Medicine, the graduates from Tamil Nadu colleges and doctors working in Tamil Nadu are admitted to the extent of 100 per cent on the basis of reservation.
- During the DMK rule to help the rural students to enjoy greater benefit, a G.O. was passed providing 15 per cent reservation for students from rural areas in Engineering and Medical colleges. As a result, for a few years a large number of students were admitted from villages. In order to spoil this, the ADMK regime increased the percentage from 15 to 25. On account of that, the Government saw to it that the matter was taken to the court and finally a situation arose when this scheme was declared null and void. We will take necessary steps to ensure that the rural students enjoy that benefit once again.
- We will find a way out to remove the practical and administrative difficulties and confusion arising out of the affiliation of all Engineering colleges to Anna University and to establish regular and quality education at all stages.
- For poor students who are not able to pay the fees in Engineering and Medical colleges, the government will pay their entire fees and hostel fees etc. and help them get education.
- We will remove the eligibility test and take steps for appointment based on university degree marks and examination conducted by Directorate of Collegiate Education.
- Teachers for appointment in primary schools will be

selected on the basis of seniority in Employment Exchange registration as was done during the DMK rule.

- Students will be provided egg twice a week on Monday and Friday along with the nutritious meal.
- In Dharmapuri, Villupuram, Perambalur, Salem and Erode where literacy rates are low, efforts will be made to provide special educational concessions and bring them on par with the educational development of other states.
- On account of the contradictions between the AICTE and UGC, in granting affiliation to Self-financing Colleges and Deemed Universities and in regulating them, Engineering students have been badly affected. Steps will be taken to see that the future of the students currently undergoing the course is not affected and approval is granted for their courses.
- Kothari Commission has noted that only if education is in the State List, it will pave way for smooth development of education. So we will take steps to get back Education exclusively in the State List.
- The Sports Department which was created during the DMK period will be reformed again and we will do the needful to make Tamil Nadu a front ranking state in sports.
- We will set up National Sports Council in Tamil Nadu.
- For each important sport, a District Headquarters will be selected and special centres will be set up for each sport.
- Every year, sports will be conducted in the state, district and Panchayat union levels and prizes will be given.
- We will distribute all the sports kits free of cost.
- We will create a situation where there will not be any District Headquarters without a stadium.

Medical Services

- We will make efforts to make Tamil Nadu Number One State in providing the best medical care by making the General Hospitals in Chennai, Coimbatore, Madurai,

Trichy, Salem and Tirunelveli, Higher Medical Research Institutes like that of the All India Institute of Medical Sciences in New Delhi.

- To prevent deadly diseases, once in three months, we will send medical teams in cooperation with NGOs to visit villages in districts, conduct medical camps, screen people and conduct tests, admit them in respective hospitals and give free medical treatment. We will take steps to provide facilities for performing heart surgery in District Headquarters hospitals, just as we have the facility in the General Hospitals in Chennai and Madurai.
- We will take steps to conduct 'AIDS' tests in all Taluk hospitals.
- Besides immediately filling all vacancies in Government hospitals, the contract system will be abolished and all those who work under that scheme will be made permanent.
- As the demand for workers relating to Medicine is increasing abroad and in our own country, we will establish educational centres in each district for conducting Para-Medical Courses.
- We will set up Special Monitoring Vigilance Cell to improve the quality of service in all Government hospitals and to monitor the medical administration system.
- We will take necessary steps for proper implementation of Child Welfare Schemes for the benefit of children affected by malnutrition with the help of NGO.

Social Justice

- We will insist on the Central Government to bring necessary amendments in the Constitution for the removal of 'Creamy Layer' concept from reservation for Backward Classes.
- We will take steps to implement 69 per cent reservation in Tamil Nadu without any impediment by expediting the case pending in the Supreme Court and trying to get an appropriate judgment.

- We will request the Central Government to amend the constitution so as to enable the State Governments to decide the quantum of reservation to SCs/STs, BCs and MBCs based on the size of their population.
- We will insist on the Central Government to implement 27 per cent reservation in admission of students in the Central Government-run IITs and other educational institutions and in the appointment of teachers as per Mandal Commission's recommendation.
- We will insist on reservation in private sector and extension of reservation in such of those Government and Public Sector Undertakings where reservation has not been implemented so far.

Employment Opportunities to the Youth

- To the educated unemployed youth, who have not got any job even after registering in Employment Exchange, unemployment allowance will be given till they get a job at the rate of Rs.150 p.m. for those who passed X standard, Rs. 200 p.m. for those who completed XII standard and Rs. 300 p.m. for graduates.
- For the youth who have been affected by the age limit ceiling and lost opportunity to get a job on account of the ban on recruitment imposed by ADMK regime, age limit will be relaxed.
- We will fill up the three lakh vacancies caused by the ban on recruitment during ADMK regime.
- As computer training is inaccessible to the youth in villages, computer instructors will be appointed in villages and a scheme of free computer training will be implemented.
- By making use of the progress, Information Technology, we will make efforts to set up I.T. Parks in Coimbatore, Trichy, Madurai, Salem, Tirunelveli and increase employment opportunities.
- We will find ways to establish Business Processing Outsourcing Centres in all districts.

Unorganised Labour Services of Welfare Boards

- We will restore and re-establish the following separate Boards which came into existence during Kalaignar's rule in 2000: Tamil Nadu Auto-rickshaw and Taxi Drivers Welfare Board, Tamil Nadu Washermen Welfare Board, Tamil Nadu Hair-dressers' Welfare Board, Tamil Nadu Tailors' Welfare Board, Handicraft Workers Welfare Board, Agricultural Labour Welfare Board, Artists Welfare Board, Footwear and Leather Processing and Producing Workers Welfare Board, Khadi and Khadi Silk Weavers Welfare Board and Stone-cutters Welfare Board etc.
- For the members of the Welfare Boards in the urorganised sector, who are above the age of 60, a pension of Rs. 300 per month will be given.

Women's Self-Help Groups

- For the training of the members of the Women Self-Help Groups, Rs. 45 was given as daily and transport allowance. But it was reduced to Rs.7.50 during Jayalalitha's regime. So the training of women was affected. As soon as the DMK Government is formed, they will be given Rs. 45 per day.
- We will resume and implement the agreement made in 1999 during Kalaignar's rule with the NGOs for giving training to the Self-Help Groups.
- We will find ways to make "Poomalai" scheme that was started during the DMK rule to market the products produced by Self-Help Groups, in cities, function in an excellent manner.
- In 1996, during DMK rule, with the help of SHGs, in many villages essential commodities are sold as a precursor. A scheme will be introduced for the distribution of essential commodities by SHGs so that the SHGs can augment their income without affecting the workers in cooperative societies under the Public Distribution System.

Self-Help Groups for the Youth

- We will introduce novel SHGs for the unemployed youth on the lines of SHGs for women.

Elections to Cooperatives

- Immediately after coming to power in 2001, Jayalalitha dissolved the Cooperative Societies. We wish to point out that though she announced that elections to cooperatives would be held within three months, in the last five years she did not conduct elections to cooperatives. We will conduct elections immediately.

Civil Supplies

Reforming Public Distribution System

- Instead of selling rice at the rate of Rs. 3.50 per kg. for the ration card holders as at present, we will distribute quality rice at the rate of Rs. 2 per kg. and bring cheers to women.
- Keeping the recreation of women and their getting general knowledge in mind, during the days of celebration of Arignar Anna's Birth Day and Thanthai Periyar's Birth Day, for those homes without a television, a scheme for distribution of free colour TV Sets will be introduced and implemented.
- For poor pregnant women, for three months before delivery and three months after delivery, maternity allowance of Rs.1000 per month will be given for six months.
- Computers will be used in the fair price shops to have transparent distribution, free from corruption.
- By converting Tamil Nadu Civil Supplies Corporation into an agent of the Food Corporation of India, and by closing direct purchase centres, Jayalalitha deprived the farmers of their livelihood. Steps will be taken to change the

situation and Civil Supplies Corporation will start procuring directly.

- We will cancel all cases filed against Civil Supplies Corporation employees out of political animosity.
- During DMK rule, with the help of Central Cooperative Bank, gas stoves were distributed to the poor. The ADMK regime initiated distraint proceedings against those poor people who were not able to pay the dues. We will cancel those dues of the poor and take steps to distribute gas stoves to the women.

Energy

- By making use of solar energy, in the remaining districts, including remote villages and hamlets, steps will be taken to provide domestic lights and street lights.

Provision of Quality Housing

- In order to provide enough housing facilities, we will implement Multi-Storeyed Housing Units Scheme.
- Just as we established sub-urban centres like Anna Nagar, Kalaignar Nagar and Maraimalai Nagar during DMK rule, no sub-urban centre was formed during the ADMK regime. Still we will form sub-urban centres with modern facilities in Chennai and other important cities like Madurai, Coimbatore, Trichy, Salem and Tirunelveli and provide all infrastructure facilities.
- We will make arrangements for granting plan approval to all the houses constructed so far without proper approval of the competent authority in all the urban areas in Tamil Nadu.
- We will extend underground drainage system to all the towns and suburban areas in Tamil Nadu.
- As it has been done in Chennai, underground cabling of electric supply will be extended to all the Corporation areas in Tamil Nadu, in the first stage.

Infrastructure Development

- We will convert all the Panchayat Union roads and Panchayat roads into quality tar roads and cement roads.
- We will convert important two lane roads of Tamil Nadu into four lane roads, and four lane roads into six lane roads, in stages.
- We will take steps to construct new bridges and over bridges in important junctions of Chennai city, taking into account the increasing vehicular traffic.
- We will take action to extend the East Coast Road from Cuddalore to Kanyakumari and gradually convert the two lane roads into four lane roads.
- We will introduce Metro Rail in Chennai and its suburban areas, as we find in the Capital Delhi and Kolkata.
- We will take action to implement rail traffic from Chennai to Mamallapuram and in the second stage extend it upto Pondicherry.
- We will undertake expansion of Anna International Airport at Chennai in a big way.
- We will upgrade the airports at Madurai, Trichy and Coimbatore. We will also improve the airports at Salem and Thoothukudi with all modern amenities.
- We will take efforts to convert the airport at Thanjavur under the control of the army, into a Civil Aerodrome.

Welfare of Adi Dravidar

- ADMK regime has ignored the Special Component Plan, which has been under implementation from the year 1980-81 with the financial support of the Central Government for the welfare of Adi Dravidar and Tribes. We will take all necessary steps to implement the Special Component Plan effectively so as to ensure that full benefits of the schemes reach the targeted groups in time.
- We will extend all concessions and scholarships to the

students who belong to Scheduled Castes and Scheduled Tribes, studying in Self-financing Engineering Colleges, Agriculture Colleges and Medical Colleges on government quota, equivalent to the education fee and hostel fee payable by them in Government Colleges.

- Sufficient number of hostels for the Adi Dravidar and Tribes will be constructed in keeping with their increasing number. All the required facilities such as adequate space, drinking water, quality food and access to internet as we find in university hostels, will be provided to them in the hostels.

Welfare of Backward Classes

- We will construct separate hostels with modern amenities for boys/girls belonging to Backward Classes, Most Backward Classes depending on the number of students.
- We will examine the demand to treat Ottar, Boyar, Pandi and Kotta as belonging to one community.

Minorities

- We will urge to fulfil the request made to the Central Government by Kalaignar M. Karunanidhi to bring in a Constitutional amendment for a separate reservation for Muslims and Christians, who are minorities, in appointments and educational institutions. We will enact a legislation providing reservation to them in Tamil Nadu.
- We will repeal the anti-conversion law, brought into force by ADMK Government.
- We will ensure that the concession now available to the Adi Dravidar are extended to all the Adi Dravidars in all the religions.

Welfare of Traders

- We will undertake tax reforms and tax restructuring to ensure continuous growth of trade and traders' welfare.

- We will enlarge the scope of Traders' Welfare Board in keeping with the demands of the changing times.
- During the DMK rule, representatives of Traders' Associations, Farmers' Associations and Government Employees Associations were invited for talks every year before the budget proposals were finalized and concessions were given to them. But in the last five years during the ADMK regime, this practice of consultations has been given up. We will again follow the practice, which was in vogue in the DMK rule.
- As VAT curtails the minimum available taxation rights of the States; creates fluctuations in Revenue income in the long run; and there is apprehension among the traders, we will not implement VAT without properly examining the implications.
- We will oppose foreign investments in retail trade; as the retail trade has become a self-employment scheme of the middle-class families.
- While the Public Sector Undertakings are functioning on profits, disposal of their shares to the private individuals should be avoided. We will protect the interest of the public sector undertakings and its shares.
- To protect the welfare of those in jewellery-making, we will impart adequate training to them and employ them as assessors in all the banks.

Welfare of Retired and Aged

- We will increase the pension amount from the present level of Rs. 200 p.m. to Rs. 400 p.m. and disburse it to the aged, physically handicapped, destitute widows and women forsaken by their husbands and there will be no ceiling on the number of beneficiaries.

Welfare of Physically Handicapped

- There was 3 per cent reservation in employment to the physically handicapped. We will insist the Central

Government to increase the percentage of reservation besides implementing the reservation strictly. The financial assistance given to them will be increased from Rs. 200 p.m. to Rs. 500 p.m.

Welfare of Weavers

- Free Electricity will be extended to the weavers in addition to the farmers.
- We will take steps to produce the raw materials for the handlooms and readymades in Tamil Nadu itself.
- We will take efforts to put up textile parks in towns like Salem, Erode, Kanchipuram, Karur and Aruppukottai.

Welfare of Fishermen

- We will take steps to prevent frequent arresting, abducting and killing of Tamil fishermen by the Sri Lankan Navy, while they go out for fishing in East Coast areas and near Kutcha Theevu.
- We will institute an enquiry into the irregularities committed in distributing financial assistance to Tsunami victims; non-distribution of financial assistance to the genuine victims and financial assistance given to the ruling partymen.
- Though the Central Government had made sufficient allocation of funds to the tsunami victims and the ADMK Government had announced that permanent houses would be constructed and handed over, so far not even a single house has been given to the affected. We will construct permanent houses and give them to all the affected families.
- We will take steps to establish fishing harbours and chilling centres necessary for the growth of fishing industry in Tamil Nadu.
- With a view to protect the welfare of "Aravanis" (Trans gender) who have been ignored and treated with disgust and contempt by all the sections of Society, we will take

appropriate decision after a thorough examination of various demands made by them.

Reorganisation of Local Bodies

- We will insist the Central Government to bring in suitable Constitutional amendment in order to remove the shortcomings and complications in the functioning of the present three-tier structure of local bodies.

Environment

- Ground water and environment are greatly affected due to uncontrolled and unlimited quarrying of sand and soil from river-beds and tanks. We will take steps to contain this trend and find alternative building-materials.
- We will encourage forestry schemes to ensure environment protection and take action to protect the unique natural wealth, birds and wildlife of the State.

Tourism Development

- Tourism is becoming an industry. We will design a master plan for tourism development as Tamil Nadu has been endowed with a long coastal line, beautiful and bewitching mountains and heritage centres of hoary art and culture.
- We will take action to run cable cars at the tourist Hill Stations like Uthagamandalam, Yercaud and Kodaikanal.
- We will encourage investments by foreign and Indian companies in the tourism sector.

Ayyan Thiruvalluvar Research Centre at Kanyakumari

- We will take action to put up Ayyan Thiruvalluvar Research Centre adjoining the Thiruvalluvar statue. Action will also be taken to make books of Tirukkural translated in various languages of the world and books of research on Tirukkural available to the visiting public.

- We will improve modern ferry services to view the Thiruvalluvar statue very closely.
- We will install Kannagi statue in the same place on the beach road where it was originally put up, as the symbol of Tamil culture, when Arignar Anna was the Chief Minister.
- We will reduce the long distance bus fares so that they are lower than the rail fares. Presently the bus fares are more than the rail fares.
- We will reduce cinema out-door shooting charges which had been hiked by Jayalalitha Government.
- We will renew and re-establish M.G.R. Film City, which had been slowly razed to the ground by Jayalalitha Government.
- We will put up a statue of "Nadigar Thilagam" Sivaji and a memorial, as it has been done by Pondicherry Government.
- DMK Government had in the past put up Manimandapam and a number of memorials for Perunthalaivar Kamarajar. We will take action to declare 15th of July, the birthday of Kamarajar, as the day of 'opening the eye of education' and organise celebrations in the schools.

Drinking Water Project

Protected Drinking Water to all;
Project for Desalination of sea water :

- In Chennai metropolitan area, drinking water problem has been continuing.
- During the DMK rule from 1996 onwards, protected drinking water was supplied to 34,428 habitations. We will implement the scheme to cover the left out habitations on a war-footing.

Tamil Nadu Legislative Council

- We will insist to bring in a constitutional amendment to

establish the Legislative Council in Tamil Nadu, as it has been done recently in Andhra Pradesh, with a view to enable the representatives of Political Pundits, Scholars, Teachers, Educationists, Employees, Lawyers, Doctors, Service organisations, Social Workers, Artists, Poets, Self-Help Groups, Traders, Farmers, Weavers and Representatives of local bodies, Labour and Fishermen associations to take part in it and advise the Government.

Welfare of Government Employees

- The concessions mercilessly withdrawn from the Government employees and teachers by the ADMK Government will be given back to them and the loss incurred by them during the strike period will be suitably compensated.
- "TESMA", brought in with a view to wreak vengeance on the Government Employees and Labour Unions will be repealed.
- When the Central Government accepted the recommendations of the Fifth Pay Commission and implemented them, the DMK Government came forward to fully accept the recommendations and implement them in respect of Tamil Nadu Government servants with retrospective effect. Likewise, we will immediately implement the recommendations of the recently-announced Sixth Pay Commission of the Government of India as an when they are formulated and released.
- We will revoke the service eligibility for full pensionary benefits which has been increased to 33 years from 30 years by the ADMK Government and fix it at 30 years and pension will be calculated on the basis of the last month's salary drawn.
- Due to atrocious action and disgusting decision of the ADMK Government, a number of Government employees, teachers, road workers and village welfare workers died of starvation and hunger. We will give financial assistance to the families of the deceased and employment to their legal heirs.

Police

- Previously during the DMK rule, Police Commission was set up twice to make recommendations for the welfare of the Police force. In the same manner, Third Police Commission will be constituted to redress the grievances of the police force and for their revival.

Social Reform Acts

- We will bring in a suitable amendment to the Act so that all trained persons from all castes can become Archakas in the temples. This was insisted by Thanthai Periyar as a principle of social reform.
- The Supreme Court of India has recently exhorted the Central and State Governments to make registration of marriages compulsory within a period of three months. We will take appropriate steps to enact a legislation in this regard.
- Kalaignar M. Karunanidhi has already sent a letter to the Prime Minister of India urging him to bring in a legislation similar to the one enacted when Arignar Anna was the Chief Minister making all the Self-Respect marriages legally valid, for the entire country. We will take follow-up action on this for an early legislation by the Government of India.
- Equality villages in memory of Thanthai Periyar were formed in the districts by the DMK rule in 1996. Social scientists lauded this scheme as a pioneering attempt to establish a society free from caste and religion. In the ADMK regime this scheme has been slighted. We will take steps to revitalise this scheme.

Marriage Assistance Scheme

- Moovalur Ramamirtham Ammaiyar Memorial Marriage Assistance Scheme implemented during the DMK rule had been stopped by the ADMK Government. The scheme will be implemented again. We will increase the financial assistance to Rs.15,000 from Rs.10,000 given earlier and we will give the increased financial assistance to the poor girls.

- It was in the DMK rule, the hand-pulled rickshaws were freely replaced with cycle rickshaws. Likewise we will put an end to the abhorrent practice of collecting human excreta by hands and give alternative employment to those doing such despicable work. Last rites— Financial assistance.
- So far financial assistance of Rs. 500 is being given to conduct the last rites of a few specific categories of poor families. This financial assistance will be enhanced to Rs. 1000 and given to all sections of society.
- We will implement the recommendations of K.P. Singh Committee, appointed by the Central Government with a view to protect the welfare of Ex-servicemen.

Transport Corporations

- The quality of service being rendered to the public by the Transport Corporations has gone down because of the administrative deterioration and corrupt practices. The Transport Corporations will be revamped and rehabilitated and we will run new buses to meet the public demand.
- We will reintroduce the Mini Bus Scheme, which was benefiting the rural students, farmers and traders during DMK rule. The routes withdrawn by the ADMK Government for the benefit of the private operators will be made operative.
- We will restore all the concessions and rights to the Transport Employees, originally given by the DMK rule and subsequently taken away by the ADMK regime.
- DMK will urge the Central Government to increase the quantum of minimum bonus from 8.33 per cent to 12 per cent and also increase the ceiling on salary.

Development Schemes for Chennai Metropolis

- During the DMK rule nine fly-overs were constructed and the work on the tenth fly-over at Perambur was started. But the ADMK regime has deliberately stopped the work at Perambur out of political hostility. We will quickly complete construction of Perambur over-bridge.
- We will implement Elevated Highway scheme in Chennai metropolis in the areas greatly affected by traffic congestion.
- We will take expeditious action to put up Multi-storeyed car parking centres in important busy locations.

Administrative and Fiscal Reforms

- Management Techniques and Methods based on the rapidly growing Information Technology are adopted in all the sectors. During the DMK rule, Right to Information Act was passed with an aim that the Government machinery adopts the latest management techniques and the administration serves the people quickly and in a transparent manner. Similar to this Act, the UPA Government at the Centre had brought into force the Right to Information Act in 2005. We propose to constitute an Administrative Reforms Committee comprising experts in various fields of public activity with a view to provide truthful and transparent administration and put into practice all the sections of the Right to Information Act. We will get the report of the committee in six months and introduce suitable reforms in administration.
- We will take all necessary steps to reorganise the industrial, fiscal and administrative sectors so as to attract large investments from within India and from abroad, in the fastly evolving global economic environment and to ensure sustainable growth in Tamil Nadu. Whenever opportunity was given to DMK in the past, it always did what it had

said and said what it had done. It took Tamil Nadu on the path of rapid growth. The DMK assures continuous and tireless service to make Tamil Nadu tread on the path of the glory again. The DMK will always live upto the expectations of the people of Tamil Nadu and fulfil their aspirations. The DMK will enhance the confidence reposed by the people of Tamil Nadu.

We will formulate growth-oriented schemes!
We will provide a very efficient administration!
We will make Tamil Nadu occupy a pride of place!
We will work vigorously following the path of ANNA!
Please support the RISING SUN!

* * *

MARVELLOUS FEATURES OF THIS MANIFESTO

- Quality Rice at Rs. 2 per kilo to make women feel happy at heart.
- Free colour TV to every family for women's recreation and general knowledge.
- Restoration of Financial Assistance for marriage—Increased to Rs.15,000.
- Rs. 45 per day as training allowance again to the members of Self-Help Groups.
- Maternity assistance to pregnant women at Rs.1000 per month for 6 months!
- Free gas stove to all poor women!
- Educational fee increased several fold will be reduced and restored to earlier level.
- With Nutritious meal to students, egg will be given twice a week.
- Monthly financial assistance upto Rs. 300 to the unemployed youth.
- Employment opportunity to three lakh youth in the vacant posts in Government departments.

- Self-Help Groups to the unemployed youth.
- Free computer Training to the youth in rural areas.
- Waiver of all cooperative loans of the farmers.
- Free electricity to Weavers in addition to farmers.
- Assignment of 2 acres of land to the landless poor families.
- Waiver of cooperative loans in the event of death of farmers!
- Selection of Teachers on the basis of registration seniority in the Employment Exchange—Among them 50 per cent will be women!
- Free electricity to farmers, who had got priority connection on payment of special deposits!
- All concessions withdrawn will be restored to Government employees and teachers.
- Financial assistance to the families of the deceased Government employees and road workers and employment to their legal heirs.
- Third Police Commission to redress the grievances of Police force and refurbish them!
- We will implement the recommendations of the Sixth Pay Commission as an when they are announced.
- All the vacancies in Government Departments, Schools, Colleges and Hospitals will be filled—The system of contract employment will be abolished.
- Separate Welfare Boards to the unorganized labour; Rs. 300 per month as pension to the members.
- Immediate provision of housing to all the fishermen and others affected by Tsunami!
- Opportunity will be given to all the trained persons from all castes to act as Archakas in the temples.
- Reservation Act for Muslims and Christians.
- Opposition to foreign investment in retail trade.
- Old age pension increased to Rs. 400.
- Physically Handicapped pension increased to Rs. 500.
- Installation of Kannagi statue in the same place, removed by the ADMK Government.
- Bus fares raised by the ADMK regime will be reduced to the level of railway fares.

- We will reduce cinema out-door shooting charges enhanced by Jayalalitha Government.
- We will re-establish MGR Film City gradually razed to the ground by Jayalalitha regime.
- We will put up early a statue and memorial for "Nadigar Thilagam" Sivaji.
- We will declare the Birth day of Kamarajar on the 15th July as the day of opening of educational eye and organise celebrations in the schools.

Annexure - V

Tamil Nadu Legislative Assembly Elections—2006.
AIADMK ELECTION MANIFESTO

Puratchi Thalaivi's Five Year Achievements (2001-2006)

- Annihilation of Forest Bandit Veerappan and his gang who challenged India's sovereignty.
- The New Veeranam Scheme successfully completed to solve the drinking water problem of Chennai Metropolis.
- Lighting the lamp of hope and confidence in the homes of farmers through the Farmers Protection Scheme.
- Free cycles to all students in Classes XI and Class XII.
- Free Textbooks for all students from Class I to Class XII.
- Annadhanam Scheme in Temples, Darghas and Churches to feed hungry mouths.
- Wasteland Development Scheme for ensuring the prosperity of the farmers.
- New Anna Marumalarchi Scheme in all Panchayat Unions with a minimum investment of Rs. 1 crore each for starting Industries, to bring smiles on the faces of the rural poor.
- Health Camps for Elephants and for the well-being of dumb creatures.
- The Namadhu Gramam Scheme for making villages self-sufficient.
- Integrated Sanitary Complexes for women.
- Total Sanitation movement.
- Protection scheme for girl children.
- Road Development Schemes.
- Drinking Water Supply Schemes.

- Irrigation Schemes.
- Upgradation of Primary Health Centres as fully equipped 30 bedded Medical Hospitals with all modern facilities and equipment.
- Formation of Women's Self-Help Groups winning the admiration of the world.
- Formation of an exclusive Women's Battalion, by the Police Department, for the first time in India.
- When the strength of women personnel in the Police Department in other States is in the range of 0.6 per cent, 1 per cent and 2 per cent, only in Tamil Nadu the percentage of Women Police personnel is more than 11 per cent— a commendable achievement of Chief Minister Puratchi Thalaivi J. Jayalalithaa.
- Entrepreneur Development Scheme for Women.
- High Technology weaving parks.
- Life Insurance Scheme for Handloom Weavers.
- Power at reduced tariff to all power looms in Tamil Nadu.
- Scheme for purchase of agricultural land for landless Adi Dravidar and Tribal women in villages.
- Rain Water Harvesting Scheme to preserve nature's bounty— an unrivalled achievement not seen anywhere else in the world.
- In order to wipe away the tears of farmers, deferment of loan repayment, waiver of interest and penal interest and settlement of loans.
- Loan at low interest rates to farmers.
- Tamil Nadu Health Development Scheme.
- Free Dhoties and Sarees for celebration of festival days.
- Distribution of Rice through Ration Shops at the lowest price in India of Rs. 3.50 per kg.
- Ration Cards for all those eligible to receive the same.
- Free Electricity scheme for hut dwellers and farmers—a facility not available in any other State in India.
- Electricity at the lowest tariff in India for Domestic Consumers.
- Own buildings for hostels for school, college students belonging to Adi Dravidar, Backward Class and Most Backward Class Communities.

- Relief for all affected by nature's devastations like Tsunami, drought, and floods.
- Series of concessions to Government employees and teachers. On behalf of the AIADMK, through the Idhayam Kappom Thittam, the lives of the poor and the indigent are being protected by Puratchi Thalaivi J. Jayalalithaa. This scheme, which no other political party in the World has thought of, is being implemented through the Puratchi Thalaivar Dr. MGR Charitable Trust for the benefit of the poor and indigent having cardiac problems. The patients are given the best of treatment in reputed private hospitals. Apart from reforming cardiac surgery, assistance towards post surgical care of the patient, including the prescribed medicines and tablets is also given — all free of cost. Further, through the *Puratchi Thalaivar Dr. MGR Charitable Trust*, Puratchi Thalaivi J. Jayalalithaa gives financial aid to poor students who are unable to pursue their studies for completing their higher education. On the occasion of May Day every year, on behalf of the All India Anna Dravida Munnetra Kazhagam's Anna Thozhirsangha Peravai, in every district organisation of the AIADMK, including the Party Organisations which function in other States, workers are selected from among the poorer sections, for giving them Rs. 25,000 each as Worker's Family Welfare Fund. Further, since Puratchi Thalaivi J. Jayalalithaa considers the cadres of the Party, as being literally its nerve and pulse, in the event of their death in an accident, each one of their families is given Rs. 50,000 or
- Rs. 1 lakh, depending on their situation. Thus Puratchi Thalaivi is wiping away the tears of sorrowing families. Puratchi Thalaivi is committed to making Tamil Nadu the Number One State in India and the people of Tamil Nadu and the AIADMK are her two eyes. As the promise of time, repository of mercy, flush with valour, and as the permanent Chief Minister of Tamil Nadu ever in the hearts and minds of our People, during Puratchi Thalaivi's rule, over the next 5 years, we look forward to :
- Escalating achievements.

- Now and forever, Tamil Nadu being maintained as a Garden of peace.
- Development of New Technology for ensuring Growth.
- The Economy scaling new heights.
- Enhancement of the quality of life of the people of Tamil Nadu.
- More developmental schemes for ensuring the welfare of the people.
- Abolition of illiteracy.
- Bettering the lives of women.
- Raising the standard of living of the poor and the indigent.
- Ensuring the prosperity of farmers, weavers, fishermen, students, Government employees, Teachers, workers and all sections of the people.
- Bringing more joy to the lives of the workers.
- To bring down prices.
- Ensuring good governance through a clean, straightforward, transparent, fast and efficient administration.
- In order to ensure continuance of the exemplary rule of Puratchi Thalaivi, to ensure prosperity for the people of Tamil Nadu and for their greater good, we seek your valuable votes so that under the leadership of Puratchi Thalaivi, the AIADMK can implement its high principles and lofty policies and continue to serve the people of Tamil Nadu, for all time, with honesty and integrity.
- With the massive support of the people of Tamil Nadu, the new Government to be headed by Puratchi Thalaivi for dispensing good government is committed to ensuring the welfare of all sections of the people, protecting their interests and that apart transforming and raising the life-style of the people of Tamil Nadu to international standards.
- For taking Tamil Nadu to its zenith, heavy funding is required to realise the enshrined rights at the State level in accordance with the prevailing Federal Structure. In keeping with these objectives MGR enunciated the formula:
- 'Neither dependence
Nor independence
But interdependence'

- So shall we go ahead bearing the above words in mind.
- Rooting out communalism, extremism and separatism which evil axis robs the people of their full life, we will gear all our efforts towards protecting the Sovereignty, Integrity and Unity of the country, making Tamil Nadu a veritable Garden of Peace.
- *Vis-à-vis* Centre-State and Inter-State issues, resolution of all such problems will be taken up in an amicable, cordial manner.
- All efforts will be taken to sanitize the onslaughts being made on Tamil Nadu's language, culture, ethos and ethnicity and thereby giving the needed thrust and impetus to ensuring a flourishing growth of Tamil literature, culture and the arts.

We pledge that we will ensure that the Tamil Nadu Police performs its duties with one hundred per cent dedication and without fear or favour in order to realise the perfect maintenance of law and public order.

- In the context of changing concepts of policing in Society, we will continue to accord the highest priority to the modernisation of the Police Force, computerisation, installing state-of-the-art communication equipment, procurement of vehicles and weapons and training programmes.
- All efforts will be taken to make Tamil Nadu the Number One State in India in Information Technology and make Tamil Nadu the cynosure of all eyes in India and the World.
- Efforts will be taken to establish greater number of IT companies in the second line cities of Tamil Nadu.
- Computer literate youth with entrepreneurial abilities will be supported in starting IT ventures.
- In the course of the next five year efforts will be taken to provide employment in the IT sector to 5 lakh youth.

The Government of Tamil Nadu will give importance to our Mother Tongue, Tamil, in Administration, Education and all communication Media. The two language formula of 'Only Tamil and English', evolved by Peraringnar Anna, will continue to be adopted as a policy. Tamil will continue to remain as the official language of Tamil Nadu, while communication with other States and the Union Government, English will be used. No imposition of any language on the people of Tamil Nadu will be permitted.

- Tamil will be used to the full in State Government offices and the subordinate Judiciary.
- Special attention will be paid to all departments and institutions pertaining to Tamil ethos and culture, like museums, the archaeological department, the Hindu Religious Endowment Board, Genesis of classical Tamil, Government Music Schools, Colleges of Art, Government College of Sculpture, Tamil Nadu's Iyal Isai Nataka Manram and the Tamil Nadu Jawahar Children Manram. All their activities will be accelerated for the continuing development of Tamil, the Tamil people and Tamil Nadu on the whole.

From 1996 to 2001, 23,125 kms. length of roads and 435 bridges alone were built. From 2001 to 2006 under Puratchi Thalaivi J. Jayalalithaa Government, 52,676 kms. length of roads and 880 bridges have been completed. In order to integrate and monitor the road projects, a Corporation called the 'Tamil Nadu Road Infrastructure Development Corporation' has been formed.

- In areas where there is congestion, grade separators will be put up to ease traffic. An investment plan to develop the infrastructure within the Chennai Metropolitan Area at a cost of Rs.18,000 crores has been finalized and is under implementation. Developmental works relating to Roads, Fly-overs, subways, road maintenance and radial roads will receive special attention. Just as the 'Namadhu Gramam' scheme of Puratchi Thalaivi J. Jayalalithaa raised the quality of life of the rural people, for the livestock of the poor and indigent in the rural areas, Puratchi Thalaivi has upgraded 317 Veterinary Sub-Centres as fullfledged Veterinary Dispensaries.

- In the course of the next five years, the 360 Veterinary Sub-Centres will be upgraded as Veterinary Dispensaries.
- The White Revolution in India was ushered in by those villages that had achieved self-sufficiency in animal husbandry activities in Tamil Nadu. 504 new Veterinary Sub-Centres will be set up in the villages of Tamil Nadu. To enable the people of rural areas to improve their economic status through Animal Husbandry programmes, special livestock maintenance camps are being conducted in the villages and hamlets. Presently in a year 5005 camps are being conducted and steps will be taken to conduct 7000 camps in a year.
- Under the Wasteland Development Scheme, importance will be given to developing pasture and green fodder and which will be made available to cattle farmers at subsidised rates.
- We will consider the implementation of a scheme of Cattle Insurance Scheme with Government subsidies towards premium. Also research will be undertaken to develop vaccines for prevention of diseases that strike goats, cows, and poultry, making Tamil Nadu a pioneer in livestock development.
- In order to provide quality animal healthcare, veterinary doctors will be imparted due training in the latest practices. Amongst the Milk producing States in India, Tamil Nadu offers the highest procurement price of Rs.12.50 per litre for Buffalo milk and Rs.10.50 per litre for cow's milk to cattle farmers. It is only in Tamil Nadu that, milk is sold to consumers at the rates ranging from Rs.11.50 to Rs.16.50 per litre depending on the milk's fat content. The number of profitably functioning Milk Producer's Co-operative Societies has increased from 3960 to 7080 over the last 5 years. During Puratchi Thalaivi J. Jayalalithaa's rule from 2001 to 2006, 3000 Milk Producers' Unions running at a loss have decreased to 465 unions. The average Milk Procurement per day which was 16.94 lakh litres has increased to 21.69 lakh litres. The average milk sales per day in the Co-operative sector has been increased to 17.32 lakh litres from 14.19 lakh litres per day. The sales of by-products of milk which was Rs. 472 crores during the DMK Regime has increased to

Rs. 932 crores because of the exemplary managerial acumen of Puratchi Thalaivi. The Clean Milk Programme was initiated at a cost of Rs.9.25 crores in order to benefit 39,000 milk producers all over the State. On the orders of Puratchi Thalaivi J. Jayalalithaa, effective from 1-6-2004, the procurement price of milk was increased by Re. 1 per litre benefiting 6 lakh milk producers in the State with an additional earning of Rs.86 crores. Puratchi Thalaivi has completely exempted from Sales Tax, Butter and Ghee produced by women in rural areas. In Tamil Nadu, 17 District Co-operative Milk Unions are functioning. Further, in the 2 districts of Perambalur and Thiruvannamalai where Milk Production is high, a Chilling Centre at Ariyalur and Chengam, and a milk powder plant at Chengam will be set up. The number of milk producers in the Co-operative fold will be increased from the existing six lakhs to seven lakhs and daily milk procurement will be increased from the present 23 lakh litres per day to 30 lakh litres per day.

- The Clean Milk Programme will be extended to all the districts in the State and bulk milk chillers will be established all over the State in order to increase the quality of the milk and to enable milk producers to get a fair price for the milk produced by them. The Government has to be brought closer to the people and a transparent administration established. This is the vision of Puratchi Thalaivi. That is why Puratchi Thalaivi is offering the benefits of IT, particularly to the people in the rural areas. The Rural Access to services through the Internet (RASI) scheme is successfully functioning in all the Districts of Tamil Nadu. The latest practices and technological developments in science, medicine and agriculture are being beemed to the villages through RASI. The computerized Land Registration Scheme 'Tamil Nilam' is functioning at all the Taluk offices. Also at every Taluk office, 'Touch Screen Kiosks' have been established, through which details pertaining to land, land valuation and birth and death can be obtained. Facilities have been made for Online Registration of small-scale industries and obtaining temporary Registration Certificates. In the Registration Department, Sub Registrar's offices have been computerized. All important cutting edge levels of administration and representatives of the people have been provided with funds to acquire computers. District Collectors and District Police Officers have been provided with Lap Top computers. The Cause list of High Courts is released daily through the Internet for the benefit of lawyers and the general public. This has enabled Tamil Nadu to be the Leader State in e-governance among the States in India.

- The Tamil Nadu State Wide Area Network (TNSWAN) facility is being implemented. This will enable connectivity at District and Taluk levels, secure the necessary detailed information for the administration to take prompt action for issuing orders. All the panchayats in Tamil Nadu have been provided computers.
- All action will be taken to transform all Government offices in Tamil Nadu into paperless offices.
- By installing Video Conferencing facilities at the Secretariat, consultation with Ministers, District Collectors and Police Chiefs is possible. This scheme will be further expanded. Poverty eradication, renovation of ponds, improvement of sanitation, food for work programme and housing facilities along with a host of other works have been undertaken in the rural areas. With the lofty aim of taking Information Technology to the villages, innovative schemes like computerisation of village Panchayats, provision of cell phones are being implemented. Throughout Tamil Nadu in all the Village Panchayats, 13,064 Integrated Sanitary Complexes for Women have been constructed at a cost of Rs. 2 lakhs each. This is a noteworthy achievement.
- The Total Sanitation Programme is implemented in all the 29 districts in Tamil Nadu. By this, Tamil Nadu has emerged as the State implementing the Total Sanitation Programme in the maximum number of Districts in the country. In line with the above achievements, constructive action will be taken to provide necessary basic amenities in all villages.

As part of the 15 Point Programme announced by the Chief Minister Puratchi Thalaivi J. Jayalalithaa, all the services pertaining to development of the urban infrastructure, supply of protected water, raising the standard of life of the urban poor, maintenance of social hygiene and Management of Solid Waste and recycling of sewage water have been given priority and are being implemented successfully. Also Municipalities and Corporations have come under the ambit of e-governance. Distribution of potable water, New underground drainage schemes, laying of storm water drains, adoption of e-governance in Municipalities, Integrated Sanitary complexes, sanitation and toilet facilities in hutment dwellings, road facilities in Municipalities and City Corporation areas, River Conservation schemes in Chennai Metro and Drinking Water Supplies in urban areas have all been implemented on an unprecedented scale.

Rain Water Harvesting Structures as Water banks

Under the Rainwater Harvesting Scheme of Tamil Nadu, a pioneering scheme as far as India is concerned, infrastructure has been developed in 1 lakh, 72 thousand 341 Government buildings, private buildings and commercial complexes, water resources, roadsides, pavements, streets, corporation tanks, bridges and mini bridges. On the whole, the Rain Water Harvesting structures covers 2.57 crore locations. This scheme will be further expanded to other required locations. The water famine faced by the people of Chennai Metro was successfully averted by the implementation of the New Veeranam Scheme at an estimated cost of Rs.720 crores, supplying 180 million litres per day drinking water.

Chennai Metro's total drinking water requirement is 840 million litres per day. To fulfil this need, Chief Minister Puratchi Thalaivi has been implementing various schemes and the New Veeranam Scheme is one of them. In order to reduce the strain on women, 39,726 mini motorized pumps have been provided to replace hand pumps. Chennai is receiving Potable water under the Krishna River Water Scheme.

9688 HDPE Sintex tanks have been purchased at a cost of Rs.15.20 crores and installed at various places in Chennai Metro. By implementing the above scheme along with utilisation of water resources and by evolving proper distribution and sharing methods all housing blocks are receiving minimum water supply in proper proportion. Schemes have been implemented for protected drinking water supply to the Municipalities, Corporations, urban areas, villages and hamlets.

Over the last 5 years, for 34 thousand 063 rural habitations supply of protected drinking water has been ensured.

39 thousand 796 mini pumpset schemes have been implemented. In order to benefit a large number of people, 256 combined Drinking Water Supply Schemes have been implemented at an estimated cost of Rs.1678 crores. In order to benefit the people in the cities, drinking water development schemes have been implemented.

In order to ensure that the people of Chennai Metro receive an assured supply of 100 million litre of water daily, a plan was conceived to set up a sea water desalination plant and all the preliminary formalities were completed. Since the Central Government's funding for the project was not forthcoming, Global tenders were invited and after consulting the Technical Experts in the field, the agency was also identified and an agreement was also concluded. When this Project was all set to be launched, deliberately enough the DMK's Union Minister for Environment refused to accord approval for the project. As a result, it has not been possible to implement the project till date.

Despite recommending to the Ministry of Environment that a team of experts be appointed by the Ministry itself to examine the project and then give its approval, the Union Minister belonging to the DMK refuses to affix just one signature in the concerned file and hence it has not been possible to commence the Project.

This is yet another example of how, the DMK Ministers at the Centre, out of their deep antipathy to Puratchi Thalaivi and with absolutely no interest in Tamil Nadu's development, continue to obstruct the project.

- Various drinking water schemes have been implemented at an estimated cost of Rs. 4,750 crores. All efforts will be taken to provide clean and protected drinking water to the people of Tamil Nadu.

- Chief Minister Puratchi Thalaivi J. Jayalalithaa's rule has placed Tamil Nadu in the top slot in Medicare among the States in India. The Madras Medical College and General Hospital have been the first in India to be awarded the ISO 9001:2000 Certificate for providing high quality medical education and medical care.
- Within the Chennai Government General Hospital, 2 new imposing hospitals blocks have been constructed, with the state of the art technology, at a cost of Rs.104.47 crores, having facilities to accommodate 2700 beds. This Hospital complex is the biggest one in Asia. The medicare offered in this hospital is much superior to the ones obtaining in Private Hospitals. The most advanced imported Medical equipment is used in the Hospital. Quality medicines are being made available here.
- In order to provide the poorer sections of society the best medical care, 300 bedded new Government Hospitals as also 12 training schools for nurses have come up at Theni, Kanniyakumari and Vellore. Orders have been issued for setting up for the first time an Ayurvedic College at Kanniyakumari. The 'Tamil Nadu Health Systems Project' has been launched to improve the health of the people especially the indigent and the disadvantaged, at a cost of Rs. 597.15 crores with financial assistance from the World Bank. In order to provide quality health care services to people from the rural areas, 106 Primary Health Centres have been upgraded as 30 bedded hospitals. These hospitals have been equipped with X-Ray equipment, ECG, Ultrasonogram, Operation theatres and Laboratories.

Another 180 Primary Health Centres provide round the clock delivery care. Accident and Emergency care facilities have been upgraded at the 10 hospitals located on the National Highways. In order to provide quality medical care to women and children, Rs. 426 crores have been allotted under the reproductive and child health care programme.

On 1-6-2005 Chief Minister Puratchi Thalaivi inaugurated at the Government Stanley Medical College the Special Scheme surgical intervention for the correction of Cleft Lip and Palate which is a congenital defect from which children suffer. This scheme has been launched for the first time in India. Under the above scheme, operation was performed on 6072 children with the congenital defect at Government Hospitals and Private Hospitals, free of cost. The operations were performed after assessing the congenital defect and upon the expressed willingness of those concerned. Thereby, Tamil Nadu has become a 'Cleft Lip and Cleft Palate Free' State. This congenital defect gives an ugly look to the child and the operation alters the face of the patient. In order to enable mothers who had lost their children in the tsunami havoc to bear children again, Chief Minister issued orders that Recanalisation Surgery be performed on those mothers, free of cost. It is for the first time in the world's history that such a scheme has been implemented.

The World Health Organisation has praised the Government of Puratchi Thalaivi J. Jayalalithaa for taking prompt action in effectively preventing the spread of infectious diseases amongst the population when tsunami, terrible rains and heavy flooding struck Tamil Nadu. For the first time in India, a birth companion scheme has been introduced, as has been ordered by Puratchi Thalaivi J. Jayalalithaa permitting one female attendant to stay with the ante-natal mother during labour.

In accordance with the orders of the Chief Minister Puratchi Thalaivi J. Jayalalithaa 4021 Doctors, 4615 Nurses and 996 Pharmacists have been appointed which is an achievement of the Government. The Government headed by Puratchi Thalaivi J. Jayalalithaa has established 62 Comprehensive Emergency Obstetric and New born care (CEmONC) Centres for providing 24 hour maternal and child health care services and these centres have been so located as to be accessible within an hour. The Government of Puratchi Thalaivi for the first time in India, has taken steps to provide medical treatment in the villages from the 885 Primary Heath Centres. A panel of doctors with all the required testing equipment would visit the villages on specified days for organising field Medical Camps.

- In Districts where there are no Medical Colleges, over the next 5 years, step by step, new Government Colleges are to be started. Also 2 new dental colleges and 21 new Nursing Colleges are to be started. The now existing 10 Nursing schools will become Nursing Colleges.
- All the Primary Health Centre will function round the clock. For that 3 Nurses and additional staff will be employed.
- The 2172 Health Centres functioning from rented premises will be provided new buildings of their own.
- Treatment will be given for snake and scorpion bites, round the clock at all the Primary Health Centres.
- All help and incentives will be given to those coming forward to start hospitals with modern facilities in villages.

Environment

In order to develop Tamil Nadu's National Wealth and to take care and protect the environment, Puratchi Thalaivi J. Jayalalithaa has been implementing a number of valuable schemes. A sum of Rs. 687.17 lakhs was spent on the National River Water Conservation Scheme. Based on the scheme, in the five cities on the banks of Cauvery River, Pollution Control measures are being undertaken by the Tamil Nadu Drinking Water Drainage Board and Local Bodies. The National Lakes Conservation Scheme, Model Eco-City, Education and creation of awareness about the environment, Institution of Awards for protection of the Environment, Development of Environment, Clean and Green roads are all pioneering Environmental Schemes that are being implemented. A proper awareness programme through modern media and traditional methods about the dangers caused by throw away plastics was undertaken. Instead of using plastic products, self-help group entrepreneurs have been given necessary training to produce Palm Leaf products.

Under the Metro River Water Conservation Scheme, there has been 100 per cent progress in pumping works and there has been 99.5 per cent progress in the purifying process for sewage water.

The Ooty and Kodaikanal lakes have been purified through employment of micro-organic technology.

- Eco restoration scheme for temple hillocks, scheme against desertification of land, Tamil Nadu Afforestation Project, Tsunami defence preparedness through coastal restoration projects including mangroves and shoreline forests and marshland renovation schemes have all been successfully implemented. These schemes will continue to be implemented.
- Industrial waste, poisonous emissions and other chemical components, apart from polluting the land, water and air, seriously affect human populations and animal life. To prevent such deleterious effects and to preserve and protect the environment, prompt action would be taken. The Government of Puratchi Thalaivi J. Jayalalithaa has won kudos for effective measures against population explosion which is the prime cause for economic decline. Several schemes have been implemented in Tamil Nadu in promoting the small family norm for effective population control. Over the last 5 years, 20 lakh 3 thousand 961 surgical operations for limiting the families have been performed.
- In order to fully realise our objective the Government of India, will be urged to allocate maximum special incentive funds to Tamil Nadu for General Medicine, Health and Women's Development. Many parents lost their children in the Tsunami disaster. Recanalisation surgeries are being offered free of cost to those parents who had undergone sterilization procedures. Rs. 25,000 per surgery is provided for surgeries in accredited private hospitals.
- The small family norm is the basis for prosperous living. In order to achieve population control Tamil Nadu has enacted a number of laws.
- Tamil Nadu's exemplary efforts in population control have contributed a great deal to national development and in this context any attempt to reduce Tamil Nadu's rightful share of Parliamentary and Assembly seats on the basis of population will be resisted. "Let us produce weapons, Produce Paper Let

us set up Factories... "FDI, a publication about International Industries reported that in 2005-2006, Tamil Nadu was the area which attracted the largest share of Industrial Investment in the world. Hitherto, New South Wales in Australia which was occupying that place was pushed to the second place after Tamil Nadu's entry, as reported by the publication. It is natural if a State Competes with States in its own country, but if it competes with other countries of the world and emerges victorious, that should indeed be considered to be a Himalayan achievement. For this, all the credit must go to Puratchi Thalaivi. Because of the excellent Law & Order situation in Tamil Nadu, the State is attracting FDI from all over the world. In Information Technology, Tamil Nadu occupies the prime position. Tamil Nadu has reached the high watermark of exporting over Rs.15 thousand crore of Software. In the Automobile sector, Tamil Nadu is virtually considered to be the 'Detroit of Asia'. Because of the efforts of Puratchi Thalaivi J. Jayalalithaa, the likes of Ford, Hyundai, Nokia, Saint-Gobain and BMW—internationally renowned companies have set up mega manufacturing centres, apart from the World Bank and the Standard Chartered Bank having set up their IT Enabled Services and Business Process Outsourcing Centres in Chennai. Further, some of the bigger international industrial houses have expressed their desire to set up industries in India. In order that infrastructure developments within the State keep pace with the needs of greater growth in Industrial Development, at an estimated cost of Rs.18 thousand cores, Chennai Metro's own infrastructure facilities i.e., roads, flyovers and supply of drinking water are in place apart from aesthetic parks dotting the various parts of the City.

A 6 way IT Express Way is being set up to attract FDI. In order to enhance industrial growth and to attract tourists, and to urge the government at the Centre to expand the Chennai's International Airports, Chief Minister Puratchi Thalaivi J. Jayalalithaa has offered free of cost 1440 acres of land. With Puratchi Thalaivi J. Jayalalithaa's exemplary industrial policy, Tamil Nadu is in the top bracket in Industrial Development. The Tamil Nadu Industrial Investment

Corporation has obtained the ISO-9001-2002 certificate from the Bureau of Indian Standards for quality management systems. In order to raise the living standards of the people in the rural areas, cities and in the districts, small-scale industries play a pioneering role. Based on this, Chief Minister Puratchi Thalaivi J. Jayalalithaa is giving priority to the growth of small-scale industries. Priority in procurement for small scale industries, temporary certificates through Internet, New Anna Marumalarchi Scheme, Backended interest subsidy for small-scale industries, Women Entrepreneurship Development Programme, Single Window System, Sale of Ooty Tea, Cashew Processing Industrial Co-operative Society.

Industrial Parks for Women, Raw Material Distribution Scheme and Marketing Assistance Schemes including that for Exports, have all been strategies devised by Chief Minister Puratchi Thalaivi J. Jayalalithaa for outstanding achievements in the sector of Small-Scale Industries. Workers act as pillars for industrial growth and the country's Economic Development. Farmers Protection Scheme, Construction Workers Welfare Scheme and Welfare Scheme for physically engaged workers have been functioning in an exemplary manner in recent years. The Industrial Sector, particularly, the Small-Scale Industries forming the base for affording long-lasting employment and help the development and ensures the efficiency of Industrial entrepreneurs. In the context of globalisation, in order to improve the productivity of small-scale units in Tamil Nadu and to modernise Industrial Units and to encourage implementation of technological development, the State Government has sponsored an interest subsidy scheme for power points.

Tamil Nadu is being talked about and compared to the Industrially fast developing countries like Brazil, Ireland and the Malaysia. This is a victory for Puratchi Thalaivi's rule, managerial acumen and tireless efforts. The previous DMK Government vide its G.O. 75 dated 19-2-1997 rescinded the price and procurement priority given to Tamil Nadu's small-scale industries and public sector undertakings. By this deplorable Government Order, the way was paved to the small-scale industries and public sector undertakings of other States to get price and procurement priority in Tamil Nadu. By this, the interests of Tamil Nadu's small-scale organisation and Public Sector Organisations were adversely affected. The products produced by the small-scale industries in Tamil Nadu were completely blocked. The DMK rule was responsible for the deterioration and closure of the small-scale industries and public sector organisations.

As soon as Puratchi Thalaivi came to power she reiterated that only if the small-scale organisations and public sector undertakings in Tamil Nadu are in a healthy State, the economy of Tamil Nadu will develop and the unemployment problem will be solved. In order to protect the interest of the small-scale organisations and public sector organisations and to enthuse them, Puratchi Thalaivi withdrew the G.O.No.75 passed by the DMK Government through a new amendment on 1-12-2001. Again on 18-11-2002 and 1-10-2004 brought amendments to the law. Also approval was given to Government organisations to procure directly the products produced by the small-scale industries and public sector industries. By this the inequity done to small-scale industries and public sector industries during the DMK rule was removed and the path was laid for their continued growth.

- All efforts will be taken to raise Tamil Nadu to greater heights in industrial development.
- With Madurai as the manufacturing hub, Virudhunagar, Ramanathapuram, Tirunelveli and Dindigul districts as Sub Manufacturing hubs, steps will be taken to start Industrial Units.
- Tuticorin will be developed as an Export Zone.
- The infrastructure of Coimbatore, Madurai, Tirunelveli, Salem, Tirunelveli will be developed like Chennai for ensuring the economic development of the surrounding villages.
- Presently the youth do not have adequate employment opportunities and have to wait for long periods of time for getting employment. In order to enthuse those seeking an occupation and those who come forward to create through their own efforts, opportunities for work in different ways, schemes will be taken up for solving the unemployment problem and for developing Industrial Manpower.
- In order to benefit disabled workers, artificial limbs, hearing

equipment and such other items will be distributed through Welfare Boards. Also, their quality of life will be improved.

- Taking into consideration the fact that for workers, housing is a basic need, loan schemes for workers will be formulated in conjunction with Banks and Financial Organisations.
- The development of science and technology rests on the small scale industries. In order to offer incentives for the small-scale sector and for the growth of industries in the villages, revolutionary schemes like New Anna Marumalarchi Thittam, Namadhu Gramam Thittam will continue to be taken up.
- Industrial Entrepreneurs are offered incentives and in order to ensure growth of exports, export service centres have been formed by the Government in District Industrial Centres for offering necessary guidance to the entrepreneurs. This service will continue to be offered.
- Small-scale units in Tamil Nadu are being given subsidies for their participation in Trade-cum-Industrial Exhibitions in other States and in other parts of the world to benefit from their exposure. These subsidies will continue to be offered. During the last DMK Rule, there was a great gap between the demand and generation of power. Because of that there were frequent power cuts.

After Puratchi Thalaivi Ammassumed Office, she took active steps to change this scenario and implemented several new schemes. This has made Tamil Nadu a surplus state in power. The peak demand reached so far in a day was 7,951 Mega Watts. The installed capacity of Tamil Nadu's Electricity Board is 10,011 Mega Watts. There is no power cut in Tamil Nadu because of implementation of schemes in a far sighted manner by Hon'ble Amma. The AIADMK Government under Hon'ble Amma generates 60 per cent of the Windmill Power in the country. This historic achievement of Puratchi Thalaivi has placed Tamil Nadu in the first place in Asia and second place in the world.

By reducing the supply of coal by 14 per cent the Central Government has put spokes in the thermal power generation. Despite this, by her sheer and administrative efficiency, Puratchi

Thalaivi Amma has ensured that there is no lag in power generation and has also made Tamil Nadu a power surplus State. For the first time in the history of Tamil Nadu, Hon'ble Chief Minister Puratchi Thalaivi Amma held direct negotiations with the employees of the Tamil Nadu Electricity Board has concluded a wage agreement acceptable to all.

Tamil Nadu has an ancient tradition of weaving and in the interest of the welfare of the handloom weavers, Hon'ble Puratchi Thalaivi Amma has formulated a number of remarkable schemes such as the provision of subsidy to handloom weavers, continuous employment opportunities, a pension scheme for weavers, a new insurance scheme for weavers and educational assistance to the wards of weavers. This has provided social and economic security to hundreds of thousands of weavers in Tamil Nadu.

- A new comprehensive scheme entitled 'The Tamil Nadu Chief Minister's Weavers Welfare Protection Scheme' will be introduced for the welfare of all weavers.
- Steps will be taken to give tax exemption to hank yarn. Hon'ble Puratchi Thalaivi Amma has formulated and implemented a number of social welfare measures for Women, Children and the Aged, which have been universally acclaimed. The Girl Child Protection Scheme, the Cradle Baby Scheme which earned the approbation of Mother Theresa, the Schemes for NGO run Hostels for Women and Homes for the Aged and Destitutes, Women's Self-Help Groups
- The development and progress of the nation depends on the development of its human resources and schemes for the welfare of the people. Comprehensive Programmes for the welfare and all-round development of all sections of society, from Infants to Senior Citizens, will continue to be formulated and implemented.
- Every effort will be made to secure 33 per cent reservation for women in Education, Employment and in institutions of Public representations.

Annexure - VI

Tamil Nadu Assembly Results

1. Mohideen Khan T.P.M. (DMK)
Margin of victory: 41,299
Total electorate 2,32,395
Votes polled 1,48,900
Mohideen Khan T.P.M. (DMK) 85,114
Nijamudeen K.M. (AIADMK) 43,815
Kaleel Raguman K.A.K.K. (DMDK) 6,342
Murugan V. (AIFB) 5,399
2001: Mohideen Khan T.P.M. (DMK) had won by 14,748

2. Velusamy S.M. (AIADMK)
Margin of victory: 5,517
Total electorate 2,36,223
Votes polled 1,67,080
Velusamy S.M. (AIADMK) 73,059
Ponmudi S.S. (DMK) 67,542
Subramaniam G. (DMDK) 19,697
Thirumurthy P.M (BJP) 3,492
2001: Velusamy S.M. (AIADMK) had won by 32,474

3. Raman E.S.S (INC)
Margin of victory: 7,315
Total electorate 1,73,462
Votes polled 1,26,680
Raman E.S.S. (INC) 58,534
Narasimhan P.M. (AIADMK) 51,219
Nethaji V. (DMDK) 10,957
Velu A. (IND) 1,490
2001: Narasimhan P.M. (AIADMK) had won by 28,240

4. Velmurugan T. (PMK)
Margin of victory: 148
Total electorate 1,75,294
Votes polled 1,43,148
Velmurugan T. (PMK) 54,653
Rajendiran R. (AIADMK) 54,505
Ramachandran S. (DMDK) 30,133
Balu S. (IND) 1,366
2001: Velmurugan T. (PMK) had won by 5,048

5. Doraikkannu R. (AIADMK)
Margin of victory: 7,001
Total electorate 1,61,259
Votes polled 1,23,180
Doraikkannu R. (AIADMK) 60,027
Ramkumar M. (INC) 53,026
Maruthaiyan N. (DMDK) 4,443
Vasudevan R. (BJP) 1,594
2001: Ramkumar M. (TMC (M)) had won by 6632

6. Ramprabhu R. (INC)
Margin of victory: 1,054
Total electorate 1,69,035
Votes polled 1,12,600
Ramprabhu R. (SC) (INC) 51,075
Sundararaj (Dr.) S. (SC) (AIADMK) 50,021
Thirumamalai Raja A. (SC) (DMDK) 4,554
UgrapandianK. (SC) (BJP) 2,090
2001: Ramprabhu R. (TMC (M)) had won by 5807

7. Srinivasan K. (AIADMK)
Margin of victory: 6,357
Total electorate 1,17,018
Votes polled 72,915
Srinivasan K. (AIADMK). 34,314
Rahmankhan A. (DMK) 27,957
Balasubramanian K. (DMDK) 5,300
Kantilal C. (BJP) 3,621
2001: Vinayakamurthi S.G. (TMC (M)) had won by 6377

8. Rengarajan N.R. (INC)
Margin of victory: 15,334
Total electorate 1,76,850
Votes polled 1,25,918
Rengarajan N.R. (INC) 58,776
Viswanathan S. (MDMK) 43,442
Senthilkumar N. (DMDK) 10,688
Jayabal P. (IND) 6,230
2001: Rengarajan N.R. (TMC (M)) had won by 6,950

9. Periannan P.N. (DMK)
Margin of victory: 26,932
Total electorate 2,08,084
Votes polled 1,49,932
Periannan P.N. (DMK) 74,109
Vetrivel S.R. (AIADMK) 47,177
Dhandapani P. (DMDK) 10,567
Muthulakshme V. (IND) 9,868
2001: Mani G.K. (PMK) had won by 14,396

10. Rajkumar M. (DMK)
Margin of victory: 6,638
Total electorate 1,81,069
Votes polled 1,33,863
Rajkumar M. (SC) (DMK) 60,478
Sundaram M. (SC) (AIADMK) 53,840
Manimegalai P. (SC) (DMDK) 12,007
Pugazhenthi C. (SC) (IND) 2,481
2001: Rajarethinam P. (AIADMK) had won by 20,004

11. Mahendran K. (CPM)
Margin of victory: 2,788
Total electorate 2,68,704
Votes polled 1,82,379
Mahendran K. (SC) (CPM) 81,765
Manimaran P. (SC) (MDMK) 78,977
Lingam J. (SC) (DMDK) 15,881
Perumal V. (SC) (BSP) 1,449
2001: Mahendran K. (CPM) had won by 17,223

12. Edirolimanian G. (PMK)
Margin of victory: 6,688
Total electorate 1,70,898
Votes polled 1,21,231
Edirolimanian G (PMK) 56,331
Anbalagan A.K.S. (AIADMK). 49,643
Gopinathan A. (DMDK) 9,149
Mani L.K. (IND) 2,105
2001: Anbalagan A.K.S. (AIADMK) had won by 8,359

13. Veerakapilan M.V.R. (AIADMK)
Margin of victory: 3,606
Total electorate 1,68,565
Votes polled 1,29,781
Veerakapilan M.V.R. (AIADMK) ... 54,183
Thirugnanasambandam S.V. (INC) 50,577
Palanivel V.S.K. (DMDK) 19,627
Thiyagarajan D. (BJP) 2,998
2001: Thirugnana Sambandham S.V. (TMC (M)) had won by 28,659

14. Panneer Selvam O. (AIADMK)
Margin of victory: 14,834
Total electorate 1,95,988
Votes polled 1,37,287
Panneer Selvam O. (AIADMK) 68,345
Mookaiah L. (DMK) 53,511
Abdul Kather M. (DMDK) 11,105
Rajapandiyan P. (BJP) 1,097
2001: Panneer Selvam O. (AIADMK) had won by 17,920

15. Chinnasamy A. (DMK)
Margin of victory: 16,915
Total electorate 1,88,544
Votes polled 1,31,491
Chinnasamy A. (SC) (DMK) 65,805
Chandra Settu S. (SC) (AIADMK)... 48,890
Kandappan H. (SC) (DMDK) 12,296
Chinnuswamy (SC) (IND) 1,527
2001: Kanagathara (Selvi) C. (AIADMK) had won by 28,855

16. Ponnudurai C. (AIADMK)
Margin of victory: 8,578
Total electorate 1,80,617
Votes polled 1,37,506
Ponnudurai C. (AIADMK) 59,631

Periyasamy N. (CPI) 51,053
Ravichandran M. (DMDK) 18,212
Shrigandheeswaran T. (BJP) 1,960
2001: Palanisamy K.S. (AIADMK) had won by 31,712

17. Velumani S.P. (AIADMK)
Margin of victory: 14,816
Total electorate 3,37,402
Votes polled 2,45,359
Velumani S.P. (AIADMK). 1,13,944
Rukumani N. (DMK) 99,128
Rajasekar S. (DMDK) 21,817
Ramamurthy K.P. (BJP) 3,906
2001: Krishnakumar M.A.P.A. alias Rohini (AIADMK) had won by 35,264

18. Pollachi Jayaraman V. (AIADMK)
Margin of victory: 2,946
Total electorate 1,93,283
Votes polled 1,35,722
Pollachi Jayaraman V. (AIADMK) 62,455
Shanthi Devi D. (DMK) 59,509
Meenakshi Sundaram.S. (DMDK) 7,543
Ragunathan V.K. (BJP) 2,039
2001: JAYARAMAN V. (AIADMK) had won by 32,404

19. Vijayakumar P. S. (INC)
Margin of victory: 7,544
Total electorate 1,73,999
Votes polled 1,24,456
Vijayakumar P.S. (INC) 58,595
Vediyappan T. (AIADMK) 51,051
Purushothaman S.C.(DMDK) 6,867
Elangeswaran G.(BJP) 2,299
2001: Nalini Manokaran (AIADMK) had won by 10,807

20. Mani S. (DMK)
Margin of victory: 53
Total electorate 1,54,491
Votes polled 1,14,351
Mani S. (DMK) 47,702
Damodaran P.V. (AIADMK). 47,649
Ramesh C. (DMDK) 7,867
Uthrakumar P. (BJP) 5,915
2001: Damodaran P.V. (AIADMK) had won by 21,815

21. Balaramanan P. (AIADMK)
Margin of victory: 11,089
Total electorate 2,48,155
Votes polled 1,75,229
Balaramanan P. (SC) (AIADMK) ... 84,259
Anbuvanan V. (SC) (DMK) 73,170
Angamuthu S. (SC) (DMDK) 13,508
Mani E. (SC) (IND) 1,649
2001: Kannan A.S. (CPI) had won by 27,390

22. Periyasamy K. (PMK)
Margin of victory: 964
Total electorate 1,61,553
Votes polled 1,20,015
Periyasamy K. (PMK) 55,375
Pounraj S. (AIADMK). 54,411
Maya Venkatesan M. (SP) 3,328
Prabakaran V.R. (DMDK) 2,395
2001: Renganathan N. (AIADMK) had won by 7,455

23. Sudarsanam D. (INC)
Margin of victory: 15,330
Total electorate 3,36,248
Votes polled 2,03,991
Sudarsanam D. (INC) 98,920
Senguttuvan R. (MDMK) 83,590
Chandrasekar G. (DMDK) 15,711
Manoharan N. (BJP) 2,062
2001: Shanmugam S. (PMK) had won by 2,316

24. Nedunchezhian R. (AIADMK)
Margin of victory: 1,950
Total electorate 2,02,027
Votes polled 1,52,502
Nedunchezhian R. (AIADMK). 64,319
Jaffarali M. (DMK) 62,369
Durai Dhiviyanathan (BJP) 13,559
Javaheer S. (DMDK) 6,880
2001: Dr. Vijayabasker.C (AIADMK) had won by 28,183

25. Babu V.S. (DMK)
Margin of victory: 7,363
Total electorate 2,94,352
Votes polled 1,91,645
Babu V.S. (DMK) 90,140
Venkateshbabu (AIADMK) 82,777
Jacquelene Gomez (DMDK) 12,690
Elumalai V. (BJP) 2,019
2001: Ranganathan B. (DMK) had won by 3,802

26. Appavu M. (DMK)
Margin of victory: 10,697
Total electorate 1,73,633
Votes polled 1,13,584
Appavu M. (DMK) 49,249
Gnanapunitha L. (AIADMK) 38,552
Selvaraj K.P.K (IND) 9,017
Sivanaintha Perumal S, (DMDK) 6,404
2001: Appavu M. (IND) had won by 18,281

27. Chandra M. (AIADMK)
Margin of victory: 493
Total electorate 2,00,783
Votes polled 1,48,122
Chandra M. (SC) (AIADMK) 58,320
Rajan V. P. (SC) (DMK) 57,827
Kalimuthu P. (SC) (BSP) 13,218
Ayyanar N. (SC) (DMDK) 10,251
2001: Rajasekar M. (AIADMK) had won by 9,595

28. Hussan Ali K. (INC)
Margin of victory: 13,367
Total electorate 2,10,426
Votes polled 1,44,149
Hussan Ali K. (INC) 66,922
Palanichamy M. (MDMK) 53,555
Dharmaraj S. (SC) (DMDK) 12,070
Sathiah A. (BJP) 5,624
2001: Anwer Rhazza A. (AIADMK) had won by 9,112

29. Gandhi R. (DMK)
Margin of victory: 32,095
Total electcrate 2,27,170
Votes polled 1,68,313
Gandhi R. (DMK) 92,584
Thamizharasan R. (AIADMK) 60,489
Paari N. (DMDK) 9,058
Shakthivel Nathan K. (IND) 1,687
2001: Chandrasekaran M.S. (AIADMK) had won by 24,963

30. Ramaswamy K.P (DMK)
Margin of victory: 4,966
Total electorate 1,87,025
Votes polled 1,37,724
Ramaswamy K.P. (DMK) 62,614
Sundaram P.R. (AIADMK) 57,648
Rajagounder R. (DMDK) 11,990
Ramasamy K. (IND) 1,490
2001: Sundaram P.R. (AIADMK) had won by 23,029

31. Sivaraj S. (INC)
Margin of victory: 7,924
Total electorate 1,86,451
Votes polled 1,28,201
Sivaraj S. (INC) 54,789
Athinarayanan L. (AIADMK) 46,865
Govindan T.K. (DMDK) 20,283
Govindaraj M. (IND) 2,757
2001: Sivaraj S. (TMC (M)) had won by 25,532

32. Jayakumar D. (AIADMK)
Margin of victory: 13,507
Total electorate 1,37,772
Votes polled 95,084
Jayakumar D. (AIADMK) 50,646
Sarkunapandian S.P. (DMK) 37,139
Royapuram V. Babu (DMDK) 5,033
Kumar V.C. (BJP) 735
2001: Jayakumar D. (AIADMK) had won by 13,712

33. Senthamizhan G. (AIADMK)
Margin of victory: 5,905
Total electorate 2,48,483
Votes polled 1,64,295
Senthamizhan G. (AIADMK) 75,973

Baskaran C.R. (PMK) 70,068
Venugopal R. (DMDK) 11,675
Ranganathan K. (SC) (BJP) 1,692
2001: Perumal V. (DMK) had won by 3,881

34. Ravichandran L. (AIADMK)
Margin of victory: 12,817
Total electorate 2,06,400
Votes polled 1,56,561
Ravichandran L. (AIADMK) 69,083
Suresh M.R. (INC) 56,266
Dhanasekar S.J. (DMDK) 27,218
Annadurai N. (BJP) 2,095
2001: Venkatajalam Se. (AIADMK) had won by 25,131

35. Arumugam S. (DMK)
Margin of victory: 14,742
Total electorate 2,50,137
Votes polled 1,80,345
Arumugam S. (DMK) 85,347
Sureshkumar R. (AIADMK) 70,605
Gnanasekaran K.V. (DMDK) 20,026
Anandhan P.T. (BJP) 1,574
2001: KARTHE M. (PMK) had won by15,085

36. Tamilarasi R. (DMK)
Margin of victory: 5,644
Total electorate 4,11,325
Votes polled 2,86,907
Tamilarasi R. (SC) (DMK) 1,24,656
Lakshmi P. (SC) (AIADMK) 1,19,012
Baskaran K. (SC) (DMDK) 35,684
Palaniveluswamy S. (SC) (BJP) 2,005
2001: Ponnampalam P. (AIADMK) had won by 19,924

37. Karuppasamy C. (AIADMK)
Margin of victory: 4,442
Total electorate 1,80,575
Votes polled 1,25,468
Karuppasamy C. (SC) (AIADMK) . 50,603
Thangavelu S. (SC) (DMK) 46,161
Karuppasamy A. (SC) (BSP) 10,015
Subbulakshmi P. (SC) (AIFB) 9,740
2001: Karuppasamy C. (AIADMK) had won by 9,262

38. Angaiyarkanni A. (Selvi) (DMK)
Margin of victory: 2,466
Total electorate 2,06,139
Votes polled 1,44,844
Angaiyarkanni A. (Selvi) (DMK) 62,970
Sanniyasi P. (AIADMK) 60,504
Chezhiyan R. (DMDK) 14,773
Annammal C. (Tmt.) (SC) (IND) 2,343
2001: Kasampu P. (PMK) had won by 1,018

39. Duraisamy V.P (DMK)
Margin of victory: 16,420
Total electorate 2,10,731
Votes polled 1,44,691
Duraisamy V.P. (SC) (DMK) 67,792
Shanthamani S. (SC) (AIADMK) ... 51,372
Easwaran R. (SC) (DMDK) 19,109
Sakthivel P. (SC) (IND) 1,918
2001: Dhanabal P. (AIADMK) had won by 22,952

40. Dharmalingam L.P. (DMK)
Margin of victory: 15,894
Total electorate 1,71,378
Votes polled 1,21,465
Dharmalingam L.P. (DMK) 56,035
Subramaniam T.K. (MDMK) 40,141
Manoharan D. (DMDK) 15,596
Sivakumar S.N.R. (BJP) 3,711
2001: Kandasamy K.R. (AIADMK) had won by 33,434

41. Rani Venkatesan (INC)
Margin of victory: 15,508
Total electorate 1,30,239
Votes polled 87,035
Rani Venkatesan (INC) 45,446
Nazareth Durai P. (MDMK) 29,938
Diamond Raja V. (DMDK) 3,827
Muthuramalingam S. (AIFB) 2,867
2001: Maninadar S.S. (TMC (M)) had won by 5,766

42. Ramachandran K.K.S.S.R. (DMK)
Margin of victory: 20,845
Total electorate 2,04,350
Votes polled 1,49,088

Ramachandran K.K.S.S.R. (DMK) 73,918
Chockeswaran G. (AIADMK) 53,073
Sankaralingam S.S.K. (DMDK) 15,391
Rajendran R. (BSP) 1,560
2001: Ramachandran K.K.S.S.R (DMK) had won by 4,415

43. Durairaj C. (AIADMK)
Margin of victory: 2,049
Total electorate 1,38,459
Votes polled 97,990
Durairaj C. (AIADMK) 42,590
Thalapathi G. (DMK) 40,541
Samundeeswari A. (DMDK) 11,099
Santhakumar K. (BJP) 1,119
2001: Durairaj C. (AIADMK) had won by 18,435

44. Ponnusamy K. (DMK)
Margin of victory: 16,534
Total electorate 1,82,451
Votes polled 1,29,240
Ponnusamy K. (ST) (DMK) 64,506
Chandran P. (ST) (AIADMK) 47,972
Santhi (Tmt) R. (ST) (DMDK) 11,747
Kuppusamy K. (ST) (BJP) 1,913
2001: Kalavathi K. (AIADMK) had won by 17,815

45. Moorthy P. (DMK)
Margin of victory: 1,586
Total electorate 1,58,021
Votes polled 1,12,702
Moorthy P. (DMK) 47,771
Santhanam L. (AIADMK) 46,185
Rajendran P. (DMDK) 13,942
Karunanidhi Pon. (BJP) 1,891
2001: Rajangam V.R. (AIADMK) had won by 19,841

46. Arul Anbarasu D. (INC)
Margin of victory: 7,916
Total electorate 1,80,495
Votes polled 1,38,112
Arul Anbarasu D. (INC) 63,502
Gopal C. (AIADMK) 55,586
Prabakaran C.D. (DMDK) 12,900
Velu V. (IND) 2,026
2001: Vilvanathan. R (AIADMK) had won by 9,795

47. Chinnaswamy R. (AIADMK)
Margin of victory: 14
Total electorate 3,37,398
Votes polled 2,40,267
Chinnaswamy R. (AIADMK) 1,00,283
Soundararajan A. (CPM) 1,00,269
Ponnusamy M. (DMDK) 31,268
Velusamy V. (BJP) 5,057
2001: KARUNAKARAN K.C. (CPM) had won by 20,001

48. Pannerselvam M. (DMK)
Margin of victory: 3,791
Total electorate 1,72,456
Votes polled 1,23,817
Pannerselvam M. (SC) (DMK) 58,609
Durairajan P. (SC) (VCK) 54,818
Balakrishnan Pon. (SC) (DMDK). 5,143
Gunasekaran N. (SC) (CPI (ML) (L)) 1,497
2001: Chandramohan N. (AIADMK) had won by 4,430

49. Gunasekaran S. (CPI)
Margin of victory: 6,113
Total electorate 1,84,172
Votes polled 1,15,675
Gunasekaran S. (CPI) 39,488
Sevanthiappan S. (MDMK) 33,375
Rajasekaran V. (IND) 30,740
Balu Cr. (DMDK) 6,114
2001: Chandran V. (AIADMK) had won by 4,273

50. Gnanadoss R. (MDMK)
Margin of victory: 9,271
Total electorate 2,53,957
Votes polled 1,83,001
Gnanadoss R. (MDMK) 79,992
Thangaraj V. (DMK) 70,721
Rajendran V. (DMDK) 12,657
Manikandan T. (AIFB) 8,329
2001: Rajagopal A. (TMC (M)) had won by 5,721

51. Yasodha D. (INC)
Margin of victory: 17,794
Total electorate 2,38,710
Votes polled 1,60,042
Yasodha D. (SC) (INC) 70,066
Balakrishnan K. (SC) (VCK) 52,272
Palani C. (SC) (DMDK) 30,096
Sivakumar G. (SC) (BJP) 2,866
2001: Yasodha D. (INC) had won by 17,193

52. Paranjothi M. (AIADMK)
Margin of victory: 10,922
Total electorate 2,59,848
Votes polled 1,93,882
Paranjothi M. (AIADMK)................ 89,135
Jerome Arokiaraj G. (INC) 78,213
Ramesh A (DMDK) 16,522
Parthiban P. (BJP) 4,878
2001: Balasubramanian.K.K (AIADMK) had won by 12676

53. Selvaraj D. (INC)
Margin of victory: 1,632
Total electorate 1,40,639
Votes polled 93,643
Selvaraj D. (INC) 38,188
Shanmuganathan S.P. (AIADMK) 36,556
Athisayakumar E. (BSP) 9,324
Sathiya Seelan C. (DMDK) 3,166
2001: Shunmuganathan S.P. (AIADMK) had won by 2,886

54. Ramasamy T. (CPI)
Margin of victory: 6,616
Total electorate 1,86,842
Votes polled 1,35,549
Ramasamy T. (CPI) 55,473
Vinayagamoorthy R. (AIADMK) ... 48,857
Dhamotharakannan R. (DMDK) 11,218
Ramaraj T. (SC) (BSP) 10,876
2001: Enbathamilan R.T. (AIADMK) had won by 9,174

55. Chinnadurai K. (DMK)
Margin of victory: 10,049
Total electorate 1,82,114
Votes polled 1,31,941
Chinnadurai K. (SC) (DMK) 60,287
Elangovan P. (SC) (AIADMK) 50,238
Geetha K. (SC) (DMDK) 12,824
Rajkumar P. (SC) (IND) 2,096
2001: Alagammal V. (AIADMK) had won by 27,857

56. Raja S.R. (DMK)
Margin of victory: 48,752
Total electorate 8,72,877
Votes polled 5,61,888
Raja S.R. (DMK) 2,69,717
Somu K. (MDMK) 2,20,965
Dharma K. (DMDK) 48,522
Sivaraman V.R. (BJP) 13,598
2001: Vaidialingam M.A. (DMK) had won by 5,431

57. Kannan P. (PMK)
Margin of victory: 12,042
Total electorate 2,00,861
Votes polled 1,41,418
Kannan P. (PMK) 48,785
Govindan P. (IND) 36,743
Thamarai Kannan K.S.V. (MDMK) 34,941
Suresh C.J. (DMDK) 14,862
2001: Kamaraj M.P. (PMK) had won by 25,458

58. Karuppasamy Pandian V. (DMK)
Margin of victory: 18,658
Total electorate 1,86,929
Votes polled 1,39,570
Karuppasamy Pandian V. (DMK) ... 69,755
Udayasuriyan Rama (MDMK) 51,097
Ravi Arunan K. (BJP) 5,190
Kamaraj S. (DMDK) 5,081
2001: Annamalai K. (AIADMK) had won by 8,792

59. Ramachandran T. (IND)
Margin of victory: 4,595
Total electorate 1,80,674
Votes polled 1,23,888
Ramachandran T. (IND) 30,032

Nagaraja Reddy P. (CPI) 25,437
Gowda N.S.M. (JD (S)) 23,628
Buttanna Y. (IND) 20,196
2001: Murali Dharan K.V. (BJP) had won by 6,217

60. Velu E.V. (DMK)
Margin of victory: 30,701
Total electorate 1,87,339
Votes polled 1,43,976
Velu E.V. (DMK) 81,592
Ramachandran S. (AIADMK) 50,891
Mohammad M. (DMDK) 4,582
Murugesan A. (IND) 1,333
2001: Velu (DMK) had won by 4,837

61. Ubayadullah S.N.M. (DMK)
Margin of victory: 10,685
Total electorate 1,85,684
Votes polled 1,22,340
Ubayadullah S.N.M. (DMK) 61,036
Rengasamy M. (AIADMK) 50,351
Sivanesan P. (DMDK) 7,477
Ramalingam M.S. (BJP) 2,051
2001: Ubayadullah S.N.M. (DMK) had won by 9,590

62. Kalairajan V.P. (AIADMK)
Margin of victory: 16,483
Total electorate 2,42,771
Votes polled 1,52,621
Kalairajan V.P. (AIADMK) 74,129
Anbazhagan J. (DMK) 57,646
Pandian T. (DMDK) 8,824
Arvind S. (LKPT) 6,323
2001: Anbazhagan J. (DMK) had won by 2,499

63. Ganesan Rd. (AIADMK)
Margin of victory: 6,983
Total electorate 2,00,448
Votes polled 1,36,690
Ganesan Rd. (AIADMK) 62,194
Dr. Rajkumar N.R.T. (INC) 55,211
Murugesan P. (DMDK) 12,425
Logandurai P. (BJP) 2,930
2001: Ganesan D (AIADMK) had won by 13,861

64. ElavarasanVeera (MDMK)
Margin of victory: 4,144
Total electorate 1,69,523
Votes polled 1,20,248
Elavarasan Veera (MDMK) 45,067
Velusamy V. (DMK) 40,923
Dhanapandiyan T. (DMDK) 19,970
Ochathevar T. (BJP) 7,790
2001: Kalimuthu K. (AIADMK) had won by 18,162

65. Subburam Rm. (INC)
Margin of victory: 314
Total electorate 1,62,477
Votes polled 1,17,986
Subburam Rm. (INC) 47,358
Radhakrishnan M. (AIADMK) 47,044
Krishnan Ku. Pa. (BJP) 10,490
Murugesan. R (DMDK) 7,863
2001: RADAKRISHNAN M. (AIADMK) had won by 12,027

66. Kumaraguru R. (AIADMK)
Margin of victory: 6,187
Total electorate 1,66,440
Votes polled 1,25,832
Kumaraguru R. (AIADMK). 57,235
Veerapandian V.S. (DMK) 51,048
Udhayakumar M.S. (DMDK) 11,366
Verapathiran M. (IND) 2,116
2001: Gnanamoorthy K.G.P. (AIADMK) had won by 14,773

67. Leema Rose R. (CPM)
Margin of victory: 28,050
Total electorate 1,65,801
Votes polled 1,10,775
Leema Rose R. (CPM) 57,162
Sujith Kumar G. (BJP) 29,112
Thilak Kumar P.C.N. (AIADMK) ... 13,363
Jeganathan D. (DMDK) 9,431
2001: Hemachandran J. (CPM) had won by 19,497

68. Sekaran K.N. (DMK)
Margin of victory: 24,762
Total electorate 2,66,993
Votes polled 1,89,750

Sekaran K.N. (DMK) 95,687
Sridhar Vandayar (AIADMK) 70,925
Thangamani K. (SC) (DMDK) 17,148
Parvathi N. (BJP) 2,007
2001: Sekaran K.N. (DMK) had won by 10,373

69. Bharathimohan R.K (AIADMK)
Margin of victory: 3,770
Total electorate 1,74,917
Votes polled 1,34,703
Bharathimohan R.K. (AIADMK) 63,233
Alayamani G. (PMK) 59,463
Sankar G. (DMDK) 5,261
Vasudevan K. (IND) 2,014
2001: Thavamani G. (AIADMK) had won by 7,372

70. Mahesh Krishnasamy T. (DMK)
Margin of victory: 1,805
Total electorate 2,00,113
Votes polled 1,49,991
Mahesh Krishnasamy T. (DMK) 69,235
Thangamuthu K. (AIADMK) 67,430
Sivakumar M. (DMDK) 8,488
Govindaraj S. (IND) 1,965
2001: Rajendran C. (AIADMK) had won by 11,223

71. Samy K.P.P. (DMK)
Margin of victory: 3,447
Total electorate 4,96,267
Votes polled 3,41,402
Samy K.P.P. (DMK) 1,58,204
Moorthy V. (AIADMK) 1,54,757
Murugan S. (DMDK) 21,915
Ganesan K. (BJP) 2,977
2001: Arumugam T. (AIADMK) had won by 34,041

72. Kannappan M. (MDMK)
Margin of victory: 9,894
Total electorate 4,20,186
Votes polled 2,96,863
Kannappan M. (MDMK). 1,23,490
Balasubramoniyan S.R. (INC) 1,13,596
Dennis Kovil Pillai E. (DMDK) 37,901
Chinnaraj M. (BJP) 13,545
2001: Balasubramoniyan S.R. (TMC (M)) had won by 28,536

73. Rajasekharan M. (INC)
Margin of victory: 53
Total electorate 1,65,785
Votes polled 1,23,642
Rajasekharan M. (INC) 43,080
Natarajan R. (MDMK) 43,027
Kannaiyan K. (IND) 17,166
Manoharan P. (DMDK) 12,445
2001: Annavi P. (AIADMK) had won by 13,148

74. Stalin M.K. (DMK)
Margin of victory: 2,468
Total electorate 1,69,506
Votes polled 1,10,299
Stalin M.K. (DMK) 49,817
Adhirajaram (AIADMK) 47,349
Thalapathy M. (DMDK) 5,545
Shri Ishrayel Maheswar A. (LKPT) ... 2,459
2001: Stalin M.K. (DMK) had won by 7,274

75. Shanmugam C.Ve. (AIADMK)
Margin of victory: 2,208
Total electorate 1,53,528
Votes polled 1,18,735
Shanmugam C.Ve. (AIADMK) 55,856
Karunanithi M. (PMK) 53,648
Lakshmanan K. (DMDK) 4,364
Manickam K. (IND) 2,102
2001: Shanmugm C.Ve. (AIADMK) had won by 12,148

76. Anitha R. Radhakrishnan (AIADMK)
Margin of victory: 13,916
Total electorate 1,66,975
Votes polled 1,11,580
Anitha R. Radhakrishnan (AIADMK) 58,600
Jeyaseelan A.D.K. (DMK) 44,684
Ganesan A. (DMDK) 3,756
Vivekanthasekar N. (IND) 1,635
2001: Anitha R. Radhakrishnan (AIADMK) had won by 11,193

77. Thanngamani P. (AIADMK)
Margin of victory: 116
Total electorate 2,96,618
Votes polled 2,12,068
Thanngamani P. (AIADMK) 85,471
Gandhiselvan S. (DMK) 85,355
Pongiyannan S. (DMDK) 32,327
Lingappan V. (IND) 2,969
2001: Ponnaiyan C. (AIADMK) had won by 44,109

78. Anbil Periasamy (DMK)
Margin of victory: 10,451
Total electorate 1,17,649
Votes polled 86,797
Anbil Periasamy (DMK) 42,886
Malarmannan A. (MDMK) 32,435
Uma P. (DMDK) 8,151
Thirumalai R. (BJP) 1,579
2001: PARANIKUMOR B. (DMK) had won by 924

79. Nehru K.N. (DMK)
Margin of victory: 16,632
Total electorate 2,11,217
Votes polled 1,49,931
Nehru K.N. (DMK) 74,026
Mariyampitchai N. (AIADMK) 57,394
Sendhureswaran A.D. (DMDK) 14,027
Mathiarasan M. (BJP) 2,413
2001: ANBIL PERIASAMY (DMK) had won by 13,944

80. Malai Raja N. (DMK)
Margin of victory: 606
Total electorate 1,98,312
Votes polled 1,42,908
Malai Raja N. (DMK) 65,517
Nainar Nagenthran (AIADMK) 64,911
Jayachandran S. (IND) 4,080
Nambirajan S. (AIFB) 2,709
2001: Nainar Nagendran (AIADMK) had won by 722

81. Bose A.K. (AIADMK)
Margin of victory: 12,686
Total electorate 3,88,164
Votes polled 2,74,014
Bose A.K. (AIADMK) 1,17,306
Venkatesan S. (CPM) 1,04,620
Rajamanickam G. (DMDK) 40,684
Surendran S. (BJP) 4,482
2001: Seenivel S.M. (AIADMK) had won by 9,127

82. Raja T.K. (PMK)
Margin of victory: 13,739
Total electorate 2,10,399
Votes polled 1,47,764
Raja T.K. (PMK) 71,932
Azhagiri K.C. (MDMK) 58,193
Senthilkumar B.S. (DMDK) 9,435
Shivashanmukam D. (BJP) 2,229
2001: Raja. T.K. (PMK) had won by 5,761

83. Periyakaruppan K.R. (DMK)
Margin of victory: 5,627
Total electorate 1,51,997
Votes polled 1,07,312
Periyakaruppan K.R. (DMK) 48,128
Umadhevan K.K. (AIADMK) 42,501
Alaguraj M. (DMDK) 12,111
Sivaraman S. (BJP) 2,029
2001: Raja T.K. (PMK) had won by 5,761

84. Moorthy D. (PMK)
Margin of victory: 10,164
Total electorate 2,47,954
Votes polled 1,62,708
Moorthy D. (SC) (PMK) 73,328
Dhanapal M. (SC) (AIADMK) 63,164
Kannappan K. (SC) (DMDK) 19,227
Ponvaratharajan M. (SC) (BJP) 1,979
2001: Kanitha Sampath S. (AIADMK) had won by 24,790

85. Govindasamy C. (CPM)
Margin of victory: 11,299
Total electorate 4,28,422
Votes polled 2,44,193
Govindasamy C. (CPM) 1,06,073
Duraisamy S. (MDMK) 94,774
Palanisamy K. (DMDK) 27,217
Karthikkeyean A.M. (BJP) 9,475
2001: Sivasami. C. (AIADMK) had won by 46,556

86. Ulaganathan K. (CPI)
Margin of victory: 22,706
Total electorate 1,80,937
Votes polled 1,37,841
Ulaganathan K. (SC) (CPI) 75,371
Umadevi A. (SC) (AIADMK) 52,665
Mohankumar K. (SC) (DMDK) 5,918
Shivashanmugam P. (SC) (BJP) 2,546
2001: Palanisamy G. (CPI) had won by 25,059

87. Hari G. (AIADMK)
Margin of victory: 916
Total electorate 1,64,790
Votes polled 1,23,192
Hari G. (AIADMK) 52,871
Eraviraj G. (PMK) 51,955
Sekar R. (DMDK) 11,293
Rajapandiyan D. (SC) (IND) 1,965
2001: Raviraj G. (PMK) had won by 13,874

88. Ramasamy K.R. (INC)
Margin of victory: 5,253
Total electorate 1,78,964
Votes polled 1,17,605
Ramasamy K.R. (INC) 55,198
Animuthu C. (AIADMK) 49,945
Thiruvengadam P. (DMDK) 6,091
Erulaiya S. (BJP) 2,064
2001: Ramasamy K.R. (TMC (M)) had won by 2,304

89. Chandrasekaran Durai (DMK)
Margin of victory: 386
Total electorate 1,49,967
Votes polled 1,14,878
Chandrasekaran Durai (DMK) 52,723
Govindarajan Durai (AIADMK) 52,337
Mahendran N. (DMDK) 6,420
Kumaravelu C. (BJP) 1,246
2001: Ayyaru Vandayar K. (AIADMK) had won by 15,689

90. Shivaji E.A.P. (DMK)
Margin of victory: 8,924
Total electorate 1,88,609
Votes polled 1,33,732
Shivaji E.A.P. (DMK) 64,378
Ramana B. (AIADMK) 55,454
Parathasarathi B. (ST) (DMDK) 8,048
Jegajeevanram S. (SC) (IND) 1,413
2001: Sudharsanam D. (TMC (M)) had won by 19,951

91. Pitchandi K. (DMK)
Margin of victory: 12,803
Total electorate 2,15,158
Votes polled 1,49,893
Pitchandi K. (DMK) 74,773
Pavan Kumar V. (AIADMK) 61,970
Kumaran S. (DMDK) 6,660
Narayana Gandhi (BJP) 1,635
2001: Pitchandi K. (DMK) had won by 4,090

92. Mathivanan U. (DMK)
Margin of victory: 26,933
Total electorate 1,76,537
Votes polled 1,35,459
Mathivanan U. (SC) (DMK) 76,901
Thangamani A. (SC) (AIADMK) 49,968
Mohankumar N. (SC) (DMDK) 5,195
Dr. Ganesan A. (SC) (BJP) 848
2001: ASOKAN A. (DMK) had won by 1,314

93. Bader Sayeed (AIADMK)
Margin of victory: 2,776
Total electorate 1,32,523
Votes polled 85,504
Bader Sayeed (AIADMK) 40,404
Naganathan M. (DMK) 37,628
Shivakumar K. (DMDK) 4,834
Sathish Kumar S. (BJP) 1,631
2001: Hussain S.A.M. (DMK) had won by 3,676

94. Geetha Jeevan P. (DMK)
Margin of victory: 15,323
Total electorate 2,42,170
Votes polled 1,57,446
Geetha Jeevan P. (DMK) 79,821
Danielraj S. (AIADMK) 64,498
Peterraj G.V. (DMDK) 7,572
Sivamurugan T. (BJP) 1,788
2001: Rajammal S. (AIADMK) had won by 16,186

95. Shanmugavelu C. (AIADMK)
Margin of victory: 3,463
Total electorate 2,07,409
Votes polled 1,43,593
Shanmugavelu C. (AIADMK) 66,178
Veluchamy C. (DMK) 62,715
Gnanasambandham G.R. (SC) (DMDK) 9,153
Kathhirvel K. (IND) 1,207
2001: Shanmugavelu C. (AIADMK) had won by 39,908

96. Thirunavukarasu K. (DMK)
Margin of victory: 18,784
Total electorate 2,14,774
Votes polled 1,49,111
Thirunavukarasu K. (SC) (DMK) ... 65,662
Vijayaraghavan E. (SC) (VCK) 46,878
Shanmugam C. (SC) (DMDK) 30,411
Ramalingam V. (SC) (BJP) 3,099
2001: Ramu N. (AIADMK) had won by 22,754

97. Rani R. (DMK)
Margin of victory: 12,382
Total electorate 1,73,935
Votes polled 1,25,957
Rani R. (ST) (DMK) 59,171
Muthusamy P. (ST) (AIADMK) 46,789
Mookan (ST) (DMDK). 14,514
Rajendran (ST) (IND) 2,066
2001: Sarojaa R. (AIADMK) had won by 12,351

98. Mahendran I. (AIADMK)
Margin of victory: 3,045
Total electorate 1,37,738
Votes polled 92,503
Mahendran I. (AIADMK) 39,009
Kathiravan P.V. (DMK) 35,964
Raja A.K.T. (DMDK) 9,672
Surendran.K (MAG) 3,874
2001: Santhanam L. (FBL) had won by 9,067

99. Sundar K. (DMK)
Margin of victory: 12,016
Total electorate 1,82,455
Votes polled 1,44,596
Sundar K. (DMK) 70,488
Somasundaram V. (AIADMK) 58,472
Murugesan D. (DMDK) 10,335
Venkatesan K.K. (IND) 2,070
2001: Somasundaram V. (AIADMK) had won by 27,622

100. Ilamathi Subramanian (AIADMK)
Margin of victory: 1,633
Total electorate 1,39,552
Votes polled 1,09,960
Ilamathi Subramanian (SC) (AIADMK) 51,939
Senthamil Chelvan S. (SC) (DMK) . 50,306
Sooriyamurthi R. (SC) (DMDK) 4,554
Anbalagan M. (SC) (IND) 1,265
2001: Boopathi Mariappan Tmt (AIADMK) had won by 23,477

101. Kovaithangam N. (INC)
Margin of victory: 20,979
Total electorate 1,27,872
Votes polled 86,321
Kovaithangam N. (SC) (INC) 46,561
Kalaiyarasan Susi S. (SC) (VCK) 25,582
Murugaraj S. (SC) (DMDK) 6,845
Thangavel M. (SC) (BJP) 2,861
2001: Kovaithangam (TMC (M)) had won by 17,915

102. Jayaraman S. P. (DMK)
Margin of victory: 22,788
Total electorate 1,74,376
Votes polled 1,23,421
Jayaraman S.P. (SC) (DMK) 65,762
Chakkrapani M. (SC) (AIADMK) .. 42,974
Sivashanmugam N. (SC) (DMDK) ... 9,096
Jayaraman S. (SC) (IND) 1,895
2001: Murugavelrajan K. (PMK) had won by 8,871

103. Abdul Basith H. (DMK)
Margin of victory: 26,184
Total electorate 1,89,807
Votes polled 1,29,360
Abdul Basith H. (DMK) 69,837
Mohamed Ali K. (AIADMK) 43,653
Anwar-Ul- Haquy K. (DMDK) 9,937
Radhakrishanan N. (IND) 2,218
2001: Abdul Latheef M. (IND) had won by 11,938

104. Ganapathy N. (AIADMK)
Margin of victory: 4,036
Total electorate 2,01,206
Votes polled 1,40,884
Ganapathy N. (SC) (AIADMK) 59,978
Soundararajan N. (SC) (PMK) 55,942
Raja K. (SC) (DMDK) 19,051
Jayapal M. (SC) (IND) 1,718
2001: Ganapathy N. (AIADMK) had won by 21,349

105. Chanthirakasi M. (AIADMK)
Margin of victory: 2,543
Total electorate 1,60,287
Votes polled 1,21,148
Chanthirakasi M. (SC) (AIADMK) 52,815
Gopalakrishnan K. (SC) (PMK) 50,272
Ganapathi M. (SC) (DMDK) 10,303
Jeeva P. (SC) (IND) 3,188
2001: Arunachalam A. (AIADMK) had won by 13,904

106. Sadhan Thirumalai Kumar (Dr.) T. (MDMK)
Margin of victory: 6,759
Total electorate 1,61,517
Votes polled 1,13,705
Sadhan Thirumalai Kumar (Dr.)(SC) (MDMK) 45,790
Krishnan R. (SC) (CPM) 39,031
Anandan D. (SC) (BSP) 14,220
Pitchai S. (SC) (DMDK) 6,390
2001: Easwaran R. (TMC (M)) had won by 11,552

107. Vedarathinam S.K. (DMK)
Margin of victory: 6,531
Total electorate 1,59,520
Votes polled 1,32,984
Vedarathinam S.K. (DMK) 66,401
Maniyan O.S. (AIADMK) 59,870
Veeravinayagam B. (DMDK) 1,708
Udayakumar M. (BJP) 1,267
2001: Vedarathinam S.K. (DMK) had won by 15,000

108. Dhandapani M. (INC)
Margin of victory: 14,758
Total electorate 2,10,197
Votes polled 1,49,370
Dhandapani M. (INC) 68,953
Palanichamy S. (AIADMK) 54,195
Venkatachalam S. (DMDK) 16,693
Paraman A. (IND) 2,263
2001: Andivel P. (AIADMK) had won by 19,126

109. Rajendran A. (DMK)
Margin of victory: 1,638
Total electorate 2,68,821
Votes polled 2,12,846
Rajendran A. (DMK) 90,477
Vijayalakshmi Palanisamy (AIADMK) 88,839
Salem Govindaraj S. (DMDK) 28,254
Annadurai A. (BJP) 1,576
2001: Selvam S.K. (AIADMK) had won by 30,012

110. Saminathan M.P. (DMK)
Margin of victory: 17,088
Total electorate 1,55,431
Votes polled 1,17,616
Saminathan M.P. (DMK) 60,909
Ganeshamurthi A. (MDMK) 43,821
Jaganathan P. (DMDK) 6,400
Vengatesh S. (IND) 1,302
2001: Saminathan M.P. (DMK) had won by 740

111. Gnanasekaran C. (INC)
Margin of victory: 21,837
Total electorate 2,07,448
Votes polled 1,35,359
Gnanasekaran C. (INC) 63,957
Subramani N. (MDMK) 42,120
Ravi G.G. (SP) 15,710
Rajenderan.A (DMDK) 9,549
2001: Gnanasekaran.C (TMC (M)) had won by 11,124

112. Chinnappan P. (AIADMK)
Margin of victory: 7,654
Total electorate 1,47,823
Votes polled 96,665
Chinnappan P. (AIADMK) 45,409

Rajaram K. (DMK) 37,755
Balakrishnan S. (DMDK) 5,279
Lingaraj (SC) (BSP) 4,026
2001: Perumal N.K. (AIADMK) had won by 15,243

113. John Joseph G. (CPM)
Margin of victory: 45,074
Total electorate 1,95,426
Votes polled 1,20,076
John Joseph G. (CPM) 64,532
Franklin F. (AIADMK) 19,458
Vijaya Raghavan Pon. (NCP) 13,434
Devadhas L. (BJP) 12,553
2001: Mony D. (CPM) had won by 22,919

114. Ranganathan B. (DMK)
Margin of victory: 30,116
Total electorate 9,41,112
Votes polled 6,11,084
Ranganathan B. (DMK) 2,78,850
Kalan G. (AIADMK) 2,48,734
Velmurugan G. (DMDK) 51,892
Ravisundaram S. (BJP) 9,202
2001: Nepoleon D. (DMK) had won by 9,230

115. Ponmudy K. (DMK)
Margin of victory: 9,748
Total electorate 2,12,630
Votes polled 1,54,636
Ponmudy K. (DMK) 72,462
Pasupathy R. (AIADMK) 62,714
Duraisamy D. (DMDK) 13,621
Vetriselvan V. (IND) 1,553
2001: Ponmudy K. (DMK) had won by 2,205

116. Varadharajan R. (MDMK)
Margin of victory: 4,107
Total electorate 1,82,473
Votes polled 1,30,333
Varadharajan R. (MDMK) 50,629
Damodaran S. (INC) 46,522
Subburaj A. (DMDK) 15,575
Selvakumaresan A. (SC) (BSP) 6,241
2001: Damodaran S. (TMC (M)) had won by 4,017

117. Vijayakanth A. (DMDK)
Margin of victory: 13,777
Total electorate 1,97,117
Votes polled 1,51,731
Vijayakanth A. (DMDK) 61,337
Govindasamy R. (PMK) 47,560
Kasinathan R. (AIADMK) 35,876
Aravind V. (BJP) 1,265
2001: Govindasamy Dr. R. (PMK) had won by 7,128

118. Tamilselvan C. (DMK)
Margin of victory: 4,107
Total electorate 1,56,742
Votes polled 1,13,627
Tamilselvan C. (ST) (DMK) 48,791
Alamelu J. (ST) (AIADMK) 44,684
Ramakrishnan V. (ST) (DMDK) 10,740
Shanmugam K. (ST) (IND) 3,073
2001: Elayakannu K.T. (AIADMK) had won by 33,985
(*Source*: Election Commission of India)

119. Sankara Valli (DMK)
Margin of victory: 15,856
Total electorate 1,46,977
Votes polled 1,09,003
Sankara Valli (SC) (DMK) 55,116
Saraswathi M. (SC) (AIADMK) 39,260
Kanthagurunathan S. (SC) (DMDK) 10,478
Balasundaram R.K. (SC) (IND) 1,926
2001: Selvaraj A. (PMK) had won by 15,478

120. Anbarasan T. M. (DMK)
Margin of victory: 17,910
Total electorate 4,31,953
Votes polled 2,84,403
Anbarasan T.M. (DMK) 1,33,232
Valarmathi B. (AIADMK) 1,15,322
Vijayakumar R. (DMDK) 22,866
Raja H. (BJP) 9,298
2001: Valarmathi B. (AIADMK) had won by 12,596

121. Rajasekaran S. (CPI)
Margin of victory: 9,151
Total electorate 1,97,744
Votes polled 1,52,986
Rajasekaran S. (CPI) 60,122
Venkatachalam A. (AIADMK) 50,971
Selvinraj K. (DMDK) 16,739
Rajaparamasivam (IND) 14,939
2001: Venkadachalam A. (AIADMK) had won by 16,731

122. Poongothai Aladiaruna (DMK)
Margin of victory: 6,845
Total electorate 1,83,349
Votes polled 1,35,294
Poongothai Aladiaruna (DMK) 62,299
Pandiaraj M. (AIADMK) 55,454
Sivakumar.M (BSP) 6,620
Samynathan.P (AIFB) 4,664
2001: Rajendran P.G. (AIADMK) had won by 4,111

123. Avudaiyappan R. (DMK)
Margin of victory: 15,381
Total electorate 1,62,742
Votes polled 1,07,604
Avudaiyappan R. (DMK) 48,972
Murugaiah Pandian R. (AIADMK) . 33,591
Narayanan A. (JD (U)) 16,325
Ponraj S. (DMDK) 2,407
2001: Sakthivel Murugan M. (AIADMK) had won by 4,020

124. Pandurangan K. (AIADMK)
Margin of victory: 53
Total electorate 1,88,557
Votes polled 1,31,558
Pandurangan K. (AIADMK) 59,220
Varalakshmi (PMK) 59,167
Venkatesan M. 7,275
Veeramani G. 1,312
2001: Pandurangan K. (AIADMK) had won by 21,051

125. Gurusamy S. (DMK)
Margin of victory: 19,240
Total electorate 1,59,908
Votes polled 1,10,203
Gurusamy S. (SC) (DMK) 56,343
Subramaniam M. (SC) (AIADMK) 37,103
Jagadeeswaran P. (SC) (DMDK) 11,498
Raju P. (SC) (IND) 1,758
2001: Krishnan R. (PMK) had won by 18,062

126. Sivasankar S.S. (DMK)
Margin of victory: 5,828
Total electorate 1,44,606
Votes polled 1,13,460
Sivasankar S.S. (DMK) 51,395
Pannerselvam K. (AIADMK) 45,567
Pannerselvam M. (DMDK) 10,954
Rajasekaran M. (BJP) 1,608
2001: Guru alias Gurunathan J. (PMK) had won by 27,002

127. Jayalalithaa J. (AIADMK)
Margin of victory: 25,186
Total electorate 1,83,610
Votes polled 1,34,304
Jayalalithaa J. (AIADMK) 73,927
Seeman (DMK) 48,741
Chandran V.S. (DMDK) 6,795
Santhakumar M. (BJP) 1,298
2001: Thanga Tamil Selvan (AIADMK) had won by 25,009

128. Arcot Veerasamy (DMK)
Margin of victory: 12,390
Total electorate 3,52,829
Votes polled 2,16,659
Arcot Veerasamy (DMK) 1,00,099
Vijaya Thayanban (MDMK) 87,709
Rajamany K. (LKPT) 11,665
Hande H.V. (BJP) 7,897
2001: Arcot Veeraswami N. (DMK) had won by 5,578

129. Udayam Shanmugam (DMK)
Margin of victory: 17,460
Total electorate 2,05,474
Votes polled 1,44,402
Udayam Shanmugam (DMK) 63,333
Karthikeyan Y. (AIADMK) 45,873
Mohamed Ali Jinnah (DMDK) 15,347
Kathamuthu Kl. (BJP) 14,713
2001: Arasan P. (MADMK) had won by 20,018

130. Khaleelur Rahman M.A. (DMK)
Margin of victory: 2,825
Total electorate 1,34,828
Votes polled 1,00,783
Khaleelur Rahman M.A. (DMK) 45,960
Monjanur Ramasamy P. (MDMK) 43,135
Basheer Mohamed A. (DMDK) 6,619
Manoharan K. (BJP) 1,744
2001: Liyaudeen Sait E.A. (AIADMK) had won by 18,326

131. Elavazhagan K.L. (PMK)
Margin of victory: 11,317
Total electorate 1,60,759
Votes polled 1,23,707
Elavazhagan K.L. (PMK) 60,286
Chandran V.R. (AIADMK) 48,969
Velu V.B. (DMDK) 8,523
Sedhumadavan S. (SP) 2,006
2001: Neelakandan P. (AIADMK) had won by 17,707

132. Amaramoorthy D. (INC)
Margin of victory: 4,194
Total electorate 1,63,907
Votes polled 1,32,460
Amaramoorthy D. (INC) 60,089
Ravichandran M. (AIADMK) 55,895
Jayavel Rama (DMDK) 8,630
Mariyappan K. (IND) 2,936
2001: Elavazhagan P. (AIADMK) had won by 10,379

133. Jaganmoorthy M. (DMK)
Margin of victory: 7,556
Total electorate 1,90,314
Votes polled 1,40,646
Jaganmoorthy M. (SC) (DMK) 66,338
Ravi S. (SC) (AIADMK) 58,782
Usha Rani R. (SC) (DMDK) 9,185
Ravi V. (SC) (IND) 2,092
2001: Bhavani Karunakaran K. (AIADMK) had won by 20,256

134. Sivanandam R. (DMK)
Margin of victory: 12,302
Total electorate 1,84,336
Votes polled 1,38,099
Sivanandam R. (DMK) 69,722
Santhanam A. (AIADMK) 57,420
Gangadharan E. (PNK) 6,292
Nallathambi R. (IND) 1,540
2001: Ramachandran K. (AIADMK) had won by 13,482

135. Thangam Thennarasu (DMK)
Margin of victory: 8,234
Total electorate 1,61,711
Votes polled 1,15,875
Thangam Thennarasu (DMK) 52,002
Murugan K. (AIADMK) 43,768
Bharathi Thasan A. (DMDK) 13,836
Krishna Ghandhi P. (AIFB) 2,234
2001: Sivasamy K.K. (AIADMK) had won by 6,152

136. Periasamy I. (DMK)
Margin of victory: 26,561
Total electorate 2,02,430
Votes polled 1,43,432
Periasamy I. (DMK) 76,308
Sreenivasan C. (AIADMK) 49,747
Rajesh Perumal P. (DMDK) 11,485
Muthuramalingam D. (BJP) 1,794
2001: Natarajaan P.K.T. (AIADMK) had won by 3,606

137. Sundaram M. R. (INC)
Margin of victory: 10,432
Total electorate 1,60,786
Votes polled 1,18,370
Sundaram M.R. (INC) 53,617
Murugesan A.K. (AIADMK) 43,185
Elangovan A.R. (DMDK) 15,654
Kumaravel A. (BJP) 1,510
2001: Murugesan A.K. (AIADMK) had won by 24,745

138. Prema R. (AIADMK)
Margin of victory: 4,994
Total electorate 1,90,450
Votes polled 1,33,961
Prema R. (SC) (AIADMK) 54,542
Arumugam M. (SC) (CPI) 49,548
Anandharaj M. (SC) (DMDK) 14,567
Mohanraj M. (SC) (IND) 11,129
2001: Mahalingam S. (AIADMK) had won by 21,012

139. Thambidurai M. (AIADMK)
Margin of victory: 3,208
Total electorate 1,97,892
Votes polled 1,43,663
Thambidurai M. (AIADMK) 61,299
Vetriselvan V. (DMK) 58,091
Govindaraj K.V. (DMDK) 11,157
Narayanasamy C. (IND) 5,666
2001: Thambidurai M. (AIADMK) had won by 49,306

140. Ramanathan K. V. (PMK)
Margin of victory: 5,103
Total electorate 1,69,720
Votes polled 1,26,612
Ramanathan K.V. (PMK) 52,603
Karuppanan K.C. (AIADMK) 47,500
Gopal P. (DMDK) 17,001
Palanisamy K.A.P. (BJP) 1,971
2001: Karuppannan K.C. (AIADMK) had won by 32,859

141. Subramaniam O. (DMK)
Margin of victory: 20,016
Total electorate 1,70,773
Votes polled 1,28,086
Subramaniam O. (DMK) 65,055
Sindu Ravichandaran (AIADMK) 45,039
Subramanian K. (DMDK) 10,399
Arumugan (SC) (IND) 2,440
2001: Chithambaram P. (AIADMK) had won by 10,275

142. Selvi Ramajayam (AIADMK)
Margin of victory: 14,823
Total electorate 1,67,859
Votes polled 1,27,834
Selvi Ramajayam (AIADMK) 65,505
Devadass K. (PMK) 50,682
Shafiuddin S. (DMDK) 7,244
Elumalai S. (BJP) 1,237
2001: Arul P.S. (IND) had won by 3,764

143. Lakshmanan, S. (DMK)
Margin of victory: 898
Total electorate 1,65,069
Votes polled 1,17,347
Lakshmanan S. (DMK) 51,474
Parthipan R. (AIADMK) 50,576
Muthuvelraj P. (IND) 5,460
Atchayakannan A. (DMDK) 4,973
2001: Ramaraj S. (AIADMK) had won by 11,278

144. Arumugam K. (PMK)
Margin of victory: 10,213
Total electorate 1,78,466
Votes polled 1,27,475
Arumugam K. (PMK) 61,664
Arumugam S. (AIADMK) 51,451
Manjula S. (DMDK) 8,852
Jeevarathinam M. (IND) 1,880
2001: Arumugam K. (PMK) had won by 5,149

145. Polur Varadhan M. (INC)
Margin of victory: 10,200
Total electorate 1,75,158
Votes polled 1,24,842
Polur Varadhan M. (SC) (INC) 53,366
Sakthivel P. (SC) (VCK) 43,166
Suresh T. (SC) (DMDK) 15,808
Thiruppathi V. (SC) (BJP) 4,009
2001: Polur Varadhan (INC) had won by 12,277

146. Karunanidhi M. (DMK)
Margin of victory: 8,522
Total electorate 1,05,252
Votes polled 67,067
Karunanidhi M. (DMK) 34,184
Dawoon Miakhan (IND) 25,662
Narayanasamy B. (DMDK) 3,681
Sivancsan. R.N. (BJP) 1,124
2001: Karunanidhi M. (DMK) had won by 4,834

147. Veldurai P. (INC)
Margin of victory: 6,032
Total electorate 1,58,911
Votes polled 1,10,996
Veldurai P. (INC) 48,527
Paul Manoj Pandian P.H. (AIADMK) 42,495

Rajendranathan S. (DMDK) 8,122
Paramasivan A. (AIFB) 5,966
2001: Paul Manoj Pandian P.H. (AIADMK) had won by 10,975

148. Vishnuprasad M. K. (INC)
Margin of victory: 4,790
Total electorate 1,69,494
Votes polled 1,35,514
Vishnuprasad M. K. (INC) 60,109
Pavai R (AIADMK) 55,319
Subamangalam D. (DMDK) 13,655
Ravichandran V. (IND) 2,369
2001: Ulagarakshagan P.S. (PMK) had won by 12,085

149. Arunmozhidevan A. (AIADMK)
Margin of victory: 16,810
Total electorate 1,47,220
Votes polled 1,11,066
Arunmozhidevan A. (AIADMK) 56,327
Balakrishnan K. (CPM) 39,517
Rajamannan P. (DMDK) 10,303
Srinivasan A. (BJP) 1,054
2001: Saravanan Durai K. (DMK) had won by 11,915

150. Udhayasooriyan T. (DMK)
Margin of victory: 20,278
Total electorate 1,79,669
Votes polled 1,32,298
Udhayasooriyan T. (DMK) 64,036
Mohan P. (AIADMK) 43,758
Subbarayalu R. (DMDK) 19,476
Mannan M.P. (SC) (IND) 1,892
2001: Mohan P. (AIADMK) had won by 9,112

151. Pongalur Palanisamy N. (DMK)
Margin of victory: 6,336
Total electorate 1,57,364
Votes polled 1,09,103
Pongalur Palanisamy N. (DMK) 51,827
Gopalakrishnan V. (AIADMK) 45,491
Mary G. (DMDK) 7,886
Shanmugam K. (BJP) 2,651
2001: Lakshmanan V.K. (TMC (M)) had won by 3,211

152. Malaravan T. (AIADMK)
Margin of victory: 14,281
Total electorate 1,40,374
Votes polled 1,00,669
Malaravan T. (AIADMK) 49,957
Maheswari A.S. (INC) 35,676
Akbar A.S. (DMDK) 8,329
Karumuthuthiagarajan M. (BJP) 4,564
2001: Maheswari S. (INC) had won by 10,091

153. Jeyapaul S. (INC)
Margin of victory: 20,997
Total electorate 1,74,762
Votes polled 1,07,323
Jeyapaul S. (INC) 50,258
Gandhi M.R (BJP) 29,261
Patchaimal K.T. (AIADMK) 20,407
Wellington S. (DMDK) 4,941
2001: Pachamal T. (AIADMK) had won by 15,089

154. Soundarapandian A. (DMK)
Margin of victory: 5,714
Total electorate 1,47,524
Votes polled 95,666
Soundarapandian A. (SC) (DMK) ... 45,303
Selvaraj M. (SC) (AIADMK) 39,589
Chidambaram.V (SC) (DMDK) 7,227
Anbarasan (Alias) Anbu D. (SC) (BJP) 1,729
2001: Kandasamy K. (TMC (M)) had won by 16,644

155. Iyappan G. (DMK)
Margin of victory: 6,266
Total electorate 1,96,095
Votes polled 1,40,286
Iyappan G. (DMK) 67,003
Kumar G. (AIADMK) 60,737
Jayakumar G.V. (DMDK) 7,866
Sivakumar P. (BJP) 1,803
2001: Pugazhendi E. (DMK) had won by 34

156. Eramakrishnan N. (MDMK)
Margin of victory: 1,958
Total electorate 1,65,427
Votes polled 1,17,390
Eramakrishnan N. (MDMK) 50,761
Selvendran P. (DMK) 48,803

Jeganath A. (DMDK) 12,360
Sakthivel A. (BJP) 2,162
2001: Ramachandran O.R. (TMC (M)) had won by 4,386

157. Prabavathi P. (DMK)
Margin of victory: 4,712
Total electorate 1,73,547
Votes polled 1,23,871
Prabavathi P. (SC) (DMK) 55,312
Ranganayahi M. (SC) (AIADMK) 50,600
Jyothipaandiyan K.N.K. (SC) (DMDK) 11,288
Santhi E. (SC) (BJP) 1,949
2001: Sivakami V. (PMK) had won by 22,152

158.Velusamy L. (PMK)
Margin of victory: 30,207
Total electorate 2,15,291
Votes polled 1,47,708
Velusamy L. (PMK) 76,195
Sampath V.S. (MDMK) 45,988
Bhaskar A. (DMDK) 17,030
Jaganathan M. (IND) 1,424
2001: Pary Mohan K. (PMK) had won by 10,974

159. Balabarathi K. (CPM)
Margin of victory: 18,949
Total electorate 2,18,221
Votes polled 1,52,748
Balabarathi K. (CPM) 66,811
Selvaragavan N. (MDMK) 47,862
Karthikeyan G. (DMDK) 27,287
Prabhakar J.C.D. (SP) 2,970
2001: Nagalakshimi K. (CPM) had won by 2,779

160. Sekar Babu P.K. (AIADMK)
Margin of victory: 18,063
Total electorate 2,39,326
Votes polled 1,67,730
Sekar Babu P.K. (AIADMK) 84,462
Manohar R. (INC) 66,399
Mohamed Jan P. (DMDK) 11,716
Prem Ananth K.P. (BJP) 1,858
2001: Sekar Babu P.K. (AIADMK) had won by 27,332

161. Kaveri V. (PMK)
Margin of victory: 6,347
Total electorate 2,22,666
Votes polled 1,69,848
Kaveri V. (PMK) 76,027
Palaniswami K. (AIADMK) 69,680
Rajendran Ak. (DMDK) 7,954
Ganesan I (IND) 6,881
2001: Ganesan I. (PMK) had won by 30,811

162. Parithi Ellamvazhuthi (DMK)
Margin of victory: 6,480
Total electorate 1,22,297
Votes polled 79,326
Parithi Ellamvazhuthi (SC) (DMK) 38,455
Sathya C.E. (SC) (MDMK) 31,975
Ethiraj. V. (SC) (DMDK) 6,031
Srirangan Prakash (SC) (BJP) 1,559
2001: Parithi.Ellamvazhuthi (DMK) had won by 86

163. Raaja Nkk. P. (DMK)
Margin of victory: 10,831
Total electorate 3,03,864
Votes polled 2,14,918
Raaja Nkk. P. (DMK) 94,938
Sivakumar E.R (AIADMK) 84,107
Chandhirakumar V.C. (DMDK) 29,011
Chairman Pon. (BJP) 1,588
2001: Thennarasu K.S. (AIADMK) had won by 24,440

164. Kannan V. (DMK)
Margin of victory: 12,933
Total electorate 1,79,189
Votes polled 1,29,946
Kannan V. (DMK) 62,350
Masilamani Dr. R. (MDMK) 49,417
Rajendran D. (DMDK) 12,491
Manivannan R. (SC) (IND) 1,670
2001: Elumalai V. (AIADMK) had won by 29,086

165. Sengottaiyan.K.A (AIADMK)
Margin of victory: 4,019
Total electorate 1,57,445
Votes polled 1,21,516

Sengottaiyan K.A (AIADMK) 55,181
V.Manimaran G.V. (DMK) 51,162
Natarajan G.S. (DMDK) 10,875
Rangasamy R. (IND) 1,518
2001: Ramaneedharan S.S. (AIADMK) had won by 28,945

166. Ramachandhiran K. (DMK)
Margin of victory: 20,232
Total electorate 2,10,699
Votes polled 1,43,372
Ramachandhiran K. (DMK) 74,147
Millar A. (AIADMK) 53,915
Krishnamurthy L. (DMDK) 7,935
Kumaran B. (BJP) 4,270
2001: A. Miller (AIADMK) had won by 32,693

167. Latha G. (CPM)
Margin of victory: 1,650
Total electorate 1,78,024
Votes polled 1,21,338
Latha G. (CPM) 48,166
Palani J.K.N. (AIADMK) 46,516
Sudhish L.K. (DMDK) 20,557
Natarajan S. (IND) 1,500
2001: Suryakala C.M. (AIADMK) had won by 24,324

168. Vijayakumar K.S. (AIADMK)
Margin of victory: 229
Total electorate 1,95,425
Votes polled 1,56,263
Vijayakumar K.S. (AIADMK). 63,147
Durai Jeyavelu (PMK) 62,918
Sekar C.H. (DMDK) 21,738
Sekar R. (IND) 2,147
2001: Sudarsanam K. (AIADMK) had won by 24,958

169. Anbazhagan K. (DMK)
Margin of victory: 409
Total electorate 1,04,115
Votes polled 60,007
Anbazhagan K. (DMK) 26,544
Seema Basheer H. (MDMK) 26,135
Chandra Prakasam C. (DMDK) 4,781
Vaithialingam V. (BJP) 1,896
2001: Anbazhagan K. (DMK) had won by 336

170. Dillibabu P. (CPM)
Margin of victory: 13,693
Total electorate 2,23,534
Votes polled 1,55,411
Dillibabu P. (SC) (CPM) 71,030
Govindasamy K. (SC) (VCK) 57,337
Arjunan P. (SC) (DMDK) 15,754
Ambethkar P. (SC) (BJP) 3,566
2001: Krishnamoorthy V (CPI) had won by 33,479

171. Gopinath K. (INC)
Margin of victory: 12,551
Total electorate 3,12,387
Votes polled 2,15,406
Gopinath K. (INC) 90,647
Sampangiramaiah V. (AIADMK) . .. 78,096
Venkatasamy B. (BJP) 23,514
Chandiran V. (DMDK) 14,401
2001: Gopinath K. (INC) had won by 6,489

172. Rajakannappan R.S. (DMK)
Margin of victory: 12,706
Total electorate 1,45,800
Votes polled 97,465
Rajakannappan R.S. (DMK) 50,952
Ayyachamy K. (AIADMK) 38,246
Manimaran V. (DMDK) 2,705
Deivendran M. (BJP) 1,344
2001: Nadarajan V.D. (AIADMK) had won by 4,682

173. Rajendran K. (AIADMK)
Margin of victory: 2,057
Total electorate 1,67,088
Votes polled 1,34,868
Rajendran K. (AIADMK) 62,001
Gurunathan J. (PMK) 59,944
Johnson M. (DMDK) 6,427
Senthamilselvi K. (IND) 1,713
2001: Annadurai S. (AIADMK) had won by 25,010

174.Thangavelan Suba. (DMK)
Margin of victory: 7,556
Total electorate 2,04,370
Votes polled 1,19,431
Thangavelan Suba. (DMK) 53,600
Sathiamoorthy V. (AIADMK). 46,044
Singai Jinnah S. (DMDK) 12,141
Sabapathy K. (SP) 2,149
2001: Balakrishnan S. (TMC (M)) had won by 6,115

175. Peter Alphonse S. (INC)
Margin of victory: 4,314
Total electorate 1,75,786
Votes polled 1,20,446
Peter Alphonse S. (INC) 53,700
Kamaludeen U.H. (AIADMK) 49,386
Arumugasamy M. (BSP) 6,760
Thiruppathy V.S. (IND) 3,229
2001: Subbiah Pandian M. (AIADMK) had won by 1,244

176. Krishnamurthy Agri S.S. (AIADMK)
Margin of victory: 7,666
Total electorate 1,81,980
Votes polled 1,42,192
Krishnamurthy Agri S.S. (AIADMK) ....
....68,586
Kalodoss R. (PMK) 60,920
Sankar L. (DMDK) 5,069
Jagadeeswaran M. (IND) 1,902
2001: Ramachandran S. (AIADMK) had won by 28,890

177. Kamalambal P. (PMK)
Margin of victory: 10,317
Total electorate 2,39,201
Votes polled 1,71,506
Kamalambal P. (PMK) 80,298
Mythili T. (AIADMK) 69,981
Eagambaram S. (DMDK) 15,158
Mari G. (IND) 2,337
2001: Thirunavukkarasu S.S. (AIADMK) had won by 23,603

178. Pushparaj S. (DMK)
Margin of victory: 7,375
Total electorate 1,86,058
Votes polled 1,39,441
Pushparaj S. (SC) (DMK) 64,620
Subramaniyan V. (SC) (AIADMK) 57,245
Rajachandra Sekar P. (SC) (DMDK) 12,509
Veeramuthu V. (SC) (IND) 1,728
2001: Subramanian V. (AIADMK) had won by 22,628

179. Sekar S. (INC)
Margin of victory: 7,296
Total electorate 1,62,590
Votes polled 1,23,559
Sekar S. (INC) 56,946
Palaniswami N.M.S. (AIADMK) 49,650
Kumarasamy P. (DMDK) 11,354
Subramaniyam K. (JD (U)) 1,883
2001: Selvi M. (AIADMK) had won by 11,274

180. Suresh Rajan N. (DMK)
Margin of victory: 10,687
Total electorate 1,76,033
Votes polled 1,26,225
Suresh Rajan N. (DMK) 63,181
Thalavai Sundaram N. (AIADMK) 52,494
Alex Shantha Sekar A. (DMDK) 5,093
Thanu Krishnan N. (BJP) 3,436
2001: Thalavaisundaram N. (AIADMK) had won by 9,536

181. Nedunchezhian K. (PMK)
Margin of victory: 8,947
Total electorate 1,71,751
Votes polled 1,22,862
Nedunchezhian K. (PMK) 58,048
Guruswamy T.N. (MDMK) 49,101
Selvi K. (DMDK) 9,576
Vijayakumar K. (IND) 1,639
2001: Malaiyappasamy A.R. (PMK) had won by 4,312

182. Sundaram N. (INC)
Margin of victory: 16,246
Total electorate 2,08,583
Votes polled 1,31,482
Sundaram N. (INC) 64,013
Venkatachalam O.L. (AIADMK) 47,767
Baskaran D. (DMDK) 13,094
Raman Nk. (BJP) 3,787
2001: Raja H. (BJP) had won by 1,651

183. Senthil Balaji V. (AIADMK)
Margin of victory: 5,384
Total electorate 2,21,389
Votes polled 1,70,676
Senthil Balaji V. (AIADMK) 80,214
Vasuki Murugesan (DMK) 74,830
Ravi A. (DMDK) 9,734
Mohan P.K. (BJP) 1,789
2001: Sivasubramanian T.N. (INC) had won by 23,438

184. Duraimurugan (DMK)
Margin of victory: 35,147
Total electorate 2,14,702
Votes polled 1,51,130
Duraimurugan (DMK) 86,824
Narayanan B. (AIADMK) 51,677
Radhakrishanan S. (DMDK) 8,492
Suresh V.R. (BJP) 1,543
2001: Duraimurugan (DMK) had won by 8,002

185. Ravikumar D. (VCK)
Margin of victory: 13,414
Total electorate 1,52,743
Votes polled 1,11,245
Ravikumar D. (SC) (VCK) 57,244
Vallalperuman P. (SC) (INC) 43,830
Umanath R. (SC) (DMDK) 6,556
Sellakkannu S. (SC) (AIVP) 902
2001: Vallalperuman P. (DMK) had won by 16,517

186. Meganathan T. A. (PMK)
Margin of victory: 11,734
Total electorate 1,83,149
Votes polled 1,41,169
Meganathan T. A. (PMK) 64,878
Munusamy K. P. (AIADMK) 53,144
Chinnaraj K. R. (DMDK) 14,892
Venkatesan V. (IND) 2,510
2001: Munusamy K.P. (AIADMK) had won by 18,517

187. John Jacob S. (INC)
Margin of victory: 26,605
Total electorate 1,54,732
Votes polled 92,455
John Jacob S. (INC) 51,016
Chandra Kumar T. (BJP) 24,411
Kumaradhas D. (AIADMK) 14,056
Richmohanraj A. (DMDK) 1,743
2001: Kumaradas Dr. (TMC (M)) had won by 13,760

188. Damodaran S. (AIADMK)
Margin of victory: 5,150
Total electorate 1,56,481
Votes polled 1,17,812
Damodaran S. (AIADMK) 55,493
Kandasamy K.V. (DMK) 50,343
Latharani C.B. (DMDK) 5,449
Muthuramalingam V. (BJP) 2,267
2001: Damodaran S. (AIADMK) had won by 33,780

189. Radhakrishnan L. (AIADMK)
Margin of victory: 12,339
Total electorate 1,76,858
Votes polled 1,14,478
Radhakrishnan L. (AIADMK). 53,354
Rajendran S. (CPI) 41,015
Srinivasaraghavan T. (DMDK) 11,633
Kovilselvan K. (SC) (BSP) 2,827
2001: Rajendran S. (CPI) had won by 9,039

190. Subramanian N. (AIADMK)
Margin of victory: 6,268
Total electorate 1,97,012
Votes polled 1,48,090
Subramanian N. (SC) (AIADMK) 68,735
Paranjothi C. (SC) (DMK) 62,467
Udayakumar M. (SC) (DMDK) 7,990
Velusamy N. (SC) (BJP) 4,827
2001: Karuppayee Dr. A. (AIADMK) had won by 46,899

191. Senguttuvan T. (DMK)
Margin of victory: 18,195
Total electorate 1,97,095
Votes polled 1,40,271
Senguttuvan T. (DMK) 69,068
Govindaraj V. (AIADMK) 50,873
Govindaraj R. (DMDK) 10,894
Davit P. (NCP) 1,913
2001: Govindarasu V. (AIADMK) had won by 21,773

192. Kamaraj P. (DMK)
Margin of victory: 8,934
Total electorate 1,61,374
Votes polled 1,26,055
Kamaraj P. (SC) (DMK) 58,394
Sasikala R. (SC) (AIADMK) 49,460
Murugan D. (SC) (DMDK) 9,728
Leelavathi M. (SC) (IND) 3,903
2001: Sasikala R. (AIADMK) had won by 21,549

193. Manickam R. (DMK)
Margin of victory: 13,989
Total electorate 1,71,539
Votes polled 1,38,070
Manickam R. (DMK) 69,615
Papasundaram A. (AIADMK) 55,626
Viswanathan M. (DMDK) 4,790
Raju N.C. (BJP) 2,010
2001: Pappasundaram A. (AIADMK) had won by 16,766

194. Mani Ko.Si. (DMK)
Margin of victory: 14,141
Total electorate 1,66,196
Votes polled 1,25,038
Mani Ko.Si. (DMK) 65,305
Eramanathan Rama (AIADMK) 51,164
Devadoss (Kuppal) G. (DMDK) 5,195
Godhandaraman R. (BJP) 1,629
2001: Mani Ko.Si. (DMK) had won by 6,496

195. Panneerselvam M.R.K. (DMK)
Margin of victory: 1,915
Total electorate 1,67,658
Votes polled 1,23,708
Panneerselvam M.R.K. (DMK) 56,462
Ramalingam N. (MDMK) 54,547
Sundaramoorthy R. (DMDK) 8,541
Saravanasundaram D. (BJP) 1,002
2001: Panneer Selvam M.R.K. (DMK) had won by 23,863

196. Anbazhagan K. Kuttalam (DMK)
Margin of victory: 11,605
Total electorate 1,67,513
Votes polled 1,29,123
Anbazhagan K. Kuttalam (DMK) ... 66,841
Rajendran S. (AIADMK) 55,236
Sarangambani K. (DMDK) 3,240
Malarvizhi D. (SC) (IND) 1,435
2001: Natarajan (AIADMK) had won by 2,644

197. Soundara Pandian A. (DMK)
Margin of victory: 3,557
Total electorate 1,74,305
Votes polled 1,32,167
Soundara Pandian A. (DMK) 62,937
Rajaram T. (AIADMK) 59,380
Ramu S. (DMDK) 4,376
Rajendran D. (BJP) 1,607
2001: Balan S.M. (AIADMK) had won by 1,610

198. Palanivelrajan T. (DMK)
Margin of victory: 7,193
Total electorate 1,35,020
Votes polled 94,224
Palanivelrajan T. (DMK) 43,185
Jakkaiyan S.T.K (AIADMK) 35,992
Sundarajan R. (DMDK) 12,038
Jeyakumar P. (IND) 949
2001: Hakeem M.A. (TMC (M)) had won by 147

199. Nanmaran N. (CPM)
Margin of victory: 52
Total electorate 1,34,455
Votes polled 95,244
Nanmaran N. (CPM) 36,384
Boominathan M. (MDMK) 36,332
Dhamodharan A. (DMDK) 18,631
Prabakaran A.P. (BJP) 1,553
2001: Nanmaran N. (CPM) had won by 5,304

200. Shanmugam S. V. (AIADMK)
Margin of victory: 3,467
Total electorate 1,85,269
Votes polled 1,31,030
Shanmugam S. V. (AIADMK) 57,208
Perumal N. (INC) 53,741
Manimaran Dr. S. (DMDK) 14,527
Bhakavathi P. (BJP) 1,851
2001: ValarmathiJebaraj (AIADMK) had won by 708

201. Ghayathri Devi K. (INC)
Margin of victory: 3,691
Total electorate 1,54,532
Votes polled 1,17,418
Ghayathri Devi K. (INC) 51,106
Appadurai K. (AIADMK) 47,415
Gajendran D. (DMDK) 9,885
Sundaramoorthy. M (BJP) 2,282
2001: Vasudevan P. (AIADMK) had won by 11,694

202. Gunasekaran M. (AIADMK)
Margin of victory: 11,455
Total electorate 1,79,349
Votes polled 1,09,458
Gunasekaran M. (SC) (AIADMK) 53,492
Paramalai K. (SC) (INC) 42,037
Mayandi P. (SC) (DMDK) 9,020
Ayyadurai R. (SC) (BJP) 1,222
2001: Paramalai K. (TMC (M)) had won by 20,857

203. Selvam K. (VCK)
Margin of victory: 6,914
Total electorate 1,93,879
Votes polled 1,42,349
Selvam K. (SC) (VCK) 62,217
Ganesan V. (SC) (DMK) 55,303
Mahadevan D. (SC) (DMDK) 15,992
Thiruvalluvan K. (SC) (IND) 2,462
2001: Thirumavalavan E.R.A. (DMK) had won by 1,855

204. Sivapunniyam V. (CPI)
Margin of victory: 6,958
Total electorate 1,83,489
Votes polled 1,37,898
Sivapunniyam V. (CPI) 68,144
Kamaraj R. (AIADMK) 61,186
Muthiya N. (DMDK) 4,500
Kalayanaraman K. (BJP) 1,894
2001: Sivapunniyam V. (CPI) had won by 20,190

205. Chinnasamy C. (AIADMK)
Margin of victory: 2,532
Total electorate 1,87,713
Votes polled 1,35,080
Chinnasamy C. (AIADMK). 57,910
Rokkaiah A. (DMK). 55,378
Kumar B.T. (BJP) 9,503
Jamal Mohamed M. (DMDK) 5,376
2001: Chelliah V.A. (AIADMK) had won by 25,272

206. Rajakumar S. (INC)
Margin of victory: 1,578
Total electorate 1,59,101
Votes polled 1,15,612
Rajakumar S. (INC) 53,490
Mahalingam M. (MDMK) 51,912
Rajendar T. Vijaya (IND) 4,346
Thavamani P. (DMDK) 2,277
2001: Veerapandian Jaga (BJP) had won by 2,452

207. Senthamizhselvan P. (PMK)
Margin of victory: 11,301
Total electorate 1,74,724
Votes polled 1,24,267
Senthamizhselvan P. (PMK) 56,758
Tamilmozhi Rajadathan (Tmt) R. (AIADMK) 45,457
Chandira Dass C. (DMDK) 15,625
Mariyappan S. (SC) (IND) 1,850
2001: Tamilmozhi R. (AIADMK) had won by 24,587

208. Samy R. (AIADMK)
Margin of victory: 3,173
Total electorate 1,90,114
Votes polled 1,35,283
Samy R. (AIADMK) 64,013
Ravichandran K.V.V. (INC) 60,840
Rajaram C.T. (DMDK) 5,269
Panneer Selvam M. (SC) (BSP) 1,292
2001: Samy R. (AIADMK) had won by 26,838

209. Chinnaraj O.K. (AIADMK)
Margin of victory: 142
Total electorate 2,04,170
Votes polled 1,51,546
Chinnaraj O.K. (AIADMK) 67,445
Arunkumar B. (DMK) 67,303
Saraswathi V. (DMDK) 10,877
Jeganathan P. (BJP) 3,187
2001: Selvaraj A.K. (AIADMK) had won by 41,078

210. Mani G. K. (PMK)
Margin of victory: 12,079
Total electorate 1,98,408
Votes polled 1,37,242
Mani G.K. (PMK) 66,250
Kandasamy K. (AIADMK) 54,171
Dhandapany S. (DMDK) 10,921
Mani M.S. (IND) 1,831
2001: Sundarambal S. (AIADMK) had won by 8,135

211. Palanisami R.M. (INC)
Margin of victory: 3,860
Total electorate 1,92,274
Votes polled 1,46,507
Palanisami R.M. (INC) 64,625
Namachivayam V.P. (AIADMK) 60,765
Victoria B. (DMDK) 10,711
Nallasamy P. (BJP) 3,303
2001: Ramasami P.C. (AIADMK) had won by 34,212

212. Mullaivendhan V. (DMK)
Margin of victory: 13,191
Total electorate 1,73,038
Votes polled 1,26,784
Mullaivendhan V. (DMK) 64,962
Singaram K. (AIADMK) 51,771
Saravanan S. (DMDK) 4,932
Pathmanapan R. (IND) 2,116
2001: Palaniappan P. (AIADMK) had won by 23,316

213. Murugavel K. (DMK)
Margin of victory: 10,521
Total electorate 1,73,271
Votes polled 1,03,706
Murugavel K. (DMK) 51,555
Kalimuthu S.P. (AIADMK) 41,034
Sivakumar M. (DMDK) 3,535
Shanmugaraj K. (SC) (BJP) 2,178
2001: Patinetampatian K. (AIADMK) had won by 2,669

214. Kaliyavarathan V.A.T. (PMK)
Margin of victory: 19,506
Total electorate 1,88,747
Votes polled 1,28,303
Kaliyavarathan V.A.T. (PMK) 46,313
Sinthanaiselvan (VCK) 26,807
Vengatesan L. (DMDK) 24,686
Sambath A.G. (IND) 21,384
2001: Gothandaraman G. (AIADMK) had won by 10,341

215. Selvaraj N. (DMK)
Margin of victory: 10,927
Total electorate 2,03,077
Votes polled 1,53,726
Selvaraj N. (DMK) 74,311
Poonachi T. P. (AIADMK) 63,384
Rajalingam M. (DMDK) 10,538
Viswanathan S. (IND) 2,037
2001: Malliga C. (AIADMK) had won by 1,994

216. Shekher S.Ve. (AIADMK)
Margin of victory: 1,657
Total electorate 2,35,246
Votes polled 1,47,335
Shekher S.Ve. (AIADMK) 62,784
Napoleon D. (DMK) 61,127
Santhanagopalan (LKPT) 9,436
Rajan V.N. (DMDK) 7,441
2001: Lakshmanan K.N. (BJP) had won by 6,047

217. Marimuthu V. (CPM)
Margin of victory: 2,344
Total electorate 1,64,819
Votes polled 1,25,060
Marimuthu V. (CPM) 57,315
Jayapal K.A. (AIADMK) 54,971
Mathiyalagan Peru (DMDK) 9,949
Karthikeyan S. (BJP) 1,758
2001: Jeevanantham R (AIADMK) had won by 16,717

218. Rajan A. (DMK)
Margin of victory: 13,745
Total electorate 1,91,270
Votes polled 1,19,390
Rajan A. (DMK) 45,354

Austin S. (IVP) 31,609
Rethinaraj S. (MDMK) 21,990
Udhaya Kumar T. (BJP) 10,752
2001: Austin (MADMK) had won by 3,662

219. Jayakumar K. (INC)
Margin of victory: 8,099
Total electorate 2,12,232
Votes polled 1,43,999
Jayakumar K. (SC) (INC) 61,306
Saradha (Tmt) R. (SC) (AIADMK) 53,207
Amudha (Tmt) P. (SC) (DMDK) 22,401
Natarajan M. (SC) (BJP) 2,178
2001: Jayakumar K. (INC) had won by 28,992

220. Vasanthakumar H. (INC)
Margin of victory: 20,075
Total electorate 1,59,393
Votes polled 1,04,665
Vasanthakumar H. (INC) 54,170
Sooriyakumar S.P. (AIADMK) 34,095
Sankar R. (AIFB) 6,869
Packia Raj I. (DMDK) 2,700
2001: Manickaraj S. (AIADMK) had won by 9,161

221. Padmavathy P. (CPI)
Margin of victory: 11,566
Total electorate 1,66,654
Votes polled 1,27,511
Padmavathy P. (SC) (CPI) 65,614
Arivanandam K. (SC) (AIADMK) 54,048
Rajendran R. (SC) (DMDK) 4,989
Rajendran S. (SC) (IND) 1,483
2001: Tamizharasan C.K. (TMC (M)) had won by 19,212

222. Viswanathan R. (AIADMK)
Margin of victory: 3,760
Total electorate 1,79,371
Votes polled 1,33,614
Viswanathan R. (AIADMK) 62,292
Andiambalam M.A. (DMK) 58,532
Ganeshan V. (DMDK) 7,754
Vedikaran P. (IND) 1,762
2001: Viswanathan R. (AIADMK) had won by 10,602

223. Sooriyakumar N.K.R. (DMK)
Margin of victory: 17,243
Total electorate 2,10,823
Votes polled 1,54,916
Sooriyakumar N.K.R. (DMK) 78,689
Subramani K.G. (AIADMK) 61,446
Fayas Basha A. (DMDK) 8,951
Pushparaj P. (BJP) 1,931
2001: Natarajan S. (PMK) had won by 12,088

224. Rajendran Saba (DMK)
Margin of victory: 12,080
Total electorate 1,64,369
Votes polled 1,24,365
Rajendran Saba (DMK) 57,403
Sabapathi Mohan R.T. (MDMK) 45,323
Sivakolunthu P. (DMDK) 15,853
Sugumaran J. (BJP) 1,160
2001: Sampath M.C. (AIADMK) had won by 7,382

225. Thenmozhi S. (AIADMK)
Margin of victory: 6,284
Total electorate 1,76,484
Votes polled 1,22,838
Thenmozhi S. (SC) (AIADMK) 53,275
Senthilvel K. (SC) (INC) 46,991
Ravichandran M. (SC) (DMDK) 16,795
Pitchaiammal P. (SC) (BJP) 1,422
2001: Anbazhagan G. (AIADMK) had won by 3,1494

226. Sakkarapani R. (DMK)
Margin of victory: 19,903
Total electorate 1,59,094
Votes polled 1,18,896
Sakkarapani R (DMK) 63,811
Nallasamy K.P. (AIADMK) 43,908
Balasubramani S. (DMDK) 5,457
Karuppusamy P. (BJP) 1,642
2001: Chakkarapani A.R.A. (DMK) had won by 13,69

227. Tamizharasu A. (PMK)
Margin of victory: 1,356
Total electorate 1,88,486
Votes polled 81,599

Tamizharasu A. (PMK) 34,888
Krishnan C. (AIADMK) 33,532
Kamalakkannan S. (DMDK) 7,195
Raja Krishnan K. (IND) 1,075
2001: Semmalai S. (AIADMK) had won by 31,602

228. Gopalan B. (INC)
Margin of victory: 4,559
Total electorate 1,50,906
Votes polled 95,797
Gopalan B. (INC) 45,551
Dorai K.N. (AIADMK) 40,992
Benjamin Jacob J. (DMDK) 4,963
Murugesan R. (BJP) 1,499
2001: Raju H.M. (INC) had won by 29,090

229. Vaithilingam R. (AIADMK)
Margin of victory: 3,843
Total electorate 1,65,978
Votes polled 1,28,638
Vaithilingam R. (AIADMK) 61,595
Rajamanickam P. (DMK) 57,752
Ramesh R. (DMDK) 7,558
Mahendran T. (BJP) 1,733
2001: Vaithilingam R. (AIADMK) had won by 19,844

230. Mohan P. (AIADMK)
Margin of victory: 9,444
Total electorate 1,44,568
Votes polled 98,404
Mohan P. (SC) (AIADMK) 38,715
Krishnasamy K. (SC) (BSP) 29,271
Rajamannar S.X. (SC) (DMK) 23,356
Mohanraj K. (SC) (DMDK) 2,690
2001: Sivaperumal A. (AIADMK) had won by 651

231. Theodare Reginald T. (DMK)
Margin of victory: 31,066
Total electorate 1,55,950
Votes polled 95,267
Theodare Reginald T. (DMK) 51,612
Rajendra Prasad K.P. (AIADMK) ... 20,546
Velayutham C. (BJP) 19,777
Selvin C. (DMDK) 1,360
2001: Raajendraprasad K.P. (AIADMK) had won by 2,774

232. Anbalagan K.P. (AIADMK)
Margin of victory: 4,844
Total electorate 1,96,330
Votes polled 1,50,902
Anbalagan K.P. (AIADMK) 66,711
Mannan K. (PMK) 61,867
Vijayashankar P. (DMDK) 11,882
Rajagopal P. (IND) 2,612
2001: Anbalagan K.P. (AIADMK) had won by 4,0232

233. Anbalakan M. (DMK)
Margin of victory: 10,909
Total electorate 1,60,854
Votes polled 1,34,786
Anbalakan M. (SC) (DMK) 57,181
Prema S. (SC) (AIADMK) 46,272
Chinnappan alias Rajendran (SC) (BJP) 16,051
Sundaram P.K. (SC) (DMDK) 11,369
2001: Chinnasamy M. (AIADMK) had won by 20,487

234. Rajendran R. (DMK)
Margin of victory: 3,889
Total electorate 2,09,051
Votes polled 1,64,238
Rajendran R. (DMK) 73,210
Elangovan R. (AIADMK) 69,321
Suresh Babu K. (DMDK) 15,802
Rajendran M. (IND) 1,606
2001: Vijayalakahmi Palanisamy P. (AIADMK) had won by 42,350

PART - II

VOTERS' REASONING OF POLITICAL PARTICIPATION

2 VOTERS' REASONING OF POLITICAL PARTICIPATION

Introduction

Who will be the next Prime Minister, Who will be the next Chief Minister, What margin? and Which party is going to be the ruling party? are interesting topics for investigation to the journalists and politicians. But to a sensitive researcher and citizen, there are other areas in election for deep exploration and interpretation. It is beyond doubt that periodic election is one of the indicators of political development[1] in the democratic polity of a country. The quality of democracy and its government is gauged not by the electoral victories of the parties and personalities but by the methodology of the political parties and the people in the conduct of election. The logic behind their voting and principles behind the approach of the political parties in the election help the democratic institutions to grow further. After five decades of democratic experience in our governance, it is heartening to note while meeting some of the voters in rural areas in certain places that the old fatalist slogan of mass "Whether Rama rules or Ravana rules, we are going to gain nothing" is vibrating in their thought, which has deeper implications and meanings and this slogan will tell upon the character and caliber of the political parties and their leaders. Some other areas who is going to give more and doles? Are the discussions among the voters which are also have deeper implications in our democracy. Against this background a study has been designed.

Statement of the Problem

This study attempts to analyse the political participation of the people in the rural areas. By political participation I refer here only the legitimate or legal acts of the individual in the society at influencing the selection of candidates for the governance of the society and more specifically the voting of the people in the general elections. The efficacy of democracy is in large part the logic with which or commitment with which the citizenry participate in the electoral process. One would find even ceremonial participation out of compulsion or as a fun. How do they understand democracy? Do they have faith in democracy? Will they express their preference based on rational calculation of the behaviour of the political parties?

In the process of political mobilization during the electioneering, the voters are placed in different stands. They are taking decisions or they are made to take decisions with regard to voting. What logic do they follow at this juncture? This is the prime questions to be investigated. It is beyond our limit in this work to traverse extensively in to the causality of the voting behaviour of people. The connection between the socio-economic status and the political activity which is one of the core areas of research in the political behaviour has no place in the present work. This study will help the students in future to embark in the area of political participation and political culture with concrete propositions.

Studies at a Glance

Studies are few in the field of Electoral politics.[2] But slowly scholars in Political Science are becoming aware of the gaps in the field and are taking up the areas for deep investigation.[3] Ramashray Roy in his trend report unequivocally analysed the substantive matter and methodology of the works that have been carried out in the domain of electoral politics. He observed that ".... in terms of substantive concerns to illustrate from election studies, it varies from an attempt to investigate into the attributes for the political system to aggregate statistical analyses of particular units in order of methodology, one finds purely impressionistic accounts, statistical descriptions and mapping operations, anthropological "indepth" analyses based on participant observation and large scale sample surveys organized around explicit conceptual frameworks for exploring both the attributes of individual voters, their cognition, perception and evaluation of certain components of the political system and the implingement on their behaviour of their socio-economic environment".[4]

General studies clearly indicated both the outcome of the election and its impact on the party system in the country. Periodical reports were also published by the election commission itself.[5] Pattern of shift has also been analysed extensively. Moreover the factors responsible for the success of parties groups and individuals are analysed.[6] More specifically certain works visualized the selection process of the candidates, campaign tactics of the individuals, groups and political parties in the election.[7] Beyond that the researchers went into the analysis of the socio economic attributes of the voters and their impact in the electoral process of the country. There are a few studies in the area of formulation of a theoretical framework brodly to analyse all the issues systematically.[8]

Having analysed all those areas Ramashray Roy listed a series of areas for further exploration and analysis. Scholars from selected centres are pursuing their research in those areas.[9] And above all daily newspapers and magazines are involved in the process of analyzing the electioneering, electoral verdict and electoral politics. Yet one area has been left unnoticed and untouched by the researchers. It is all the more important because it decides the nature of political culture. Hence logic behind voting is taken for investigation.

A country with 72 per cent of the people living in the rural areas and nearly 26 per cent of them are living below the poverty line has so far witnessed thirteen general elections. Yet it is a serious question whether the people in the course of five decades have gained substantial amount of knowledge about the democratic system. Unless the people with full commitment towards the democratic process go to the booth, the election that the country has conducted twelve times has no meaning. Hence an attempt has been made to study the people's attitude.

Theoretical Framework

Generally attempts have been made by our scholars to evolve a meaningful theory to explain the electoral behaviour. Electoral studies are abundant in the west. The studies conducted in the west[10] helped out scholars methodologically to pursue their studies in electoral behaviour. Though many attempts had been initiated, most of them are half way through. A few started with a premise and ended with a note of limitation with out fulfilling the objectives. This study takes its premises not from the theoretical works on election or electoral politics but it goes to the root of democratic polity, political culture. It is both a micro as well as a macro study. First, Graham Wallahs in his book "Human Nature in Politics" indicated the failure of the students of politics. Students of Politics studies the political behaviour of the institutions and not the man responsible for the behaviour of the Institutions.[11] Following the observation of Graham Wallahs, a large number of scholars embarked on the analysis of man. By analyzing the roots of our democracy we can give a meaningful explanation and interpretation to the electoral behaviour of the people and the parties.

While considering the political culture, it is very difficult to fix the Indian society as a whole in an one of the types of political culture since it has got a good mixture of ethnic groups. Likewise it is highly difficult to fix the nature of orientation of the human collectivities in the Indian society. It has got grouped having a variety of political culture from tribal political culture to participant political culture. But when one takes a model value, Indian political culture would fall in the category of a combination of tribal and subject political culture. To test the proposition whether India has got maturity of keeping the country in democratic tradition, this study would help immensely. Basically, for any rational political action one has got the awareness of the political events in the context of the output functions of the political system. Apart from the awareness and evaluation, the member has to identify with an ideology for his/her political action. Thus for a meaningful political participation the people have to be oriented in three dimensions namely cognitive orientation, affection orientation, and evaluative orientation.[12] With this background, the people's rationale behind their participation in the electoral competition is analysed.

Measures of Political Participation

Earlier studies conducted by the scholars like Julian L. Woodward and Elmo Roper highlighted the indicators of political participation by the members of society.[13] Participation would be possible through different channels. The Channels are (a) Voting at the poll; (b) Supporting groups or parties through their membership; (c) Personally contacting the politicians for all political actions; (d) Participating in all meeting of the parties; (e) Communicating all messages to the other fellow citizens about the political process. But following the Index of political participation, community studies have been conducted.[14]

Methodology

This study is based on a combination of a survey and participant observation. The principle investigator had made several visits to the villages frequently and had a close interaction with the voters. Primarily the study though guided by theoretical premises, the major substantive aspect has been taken for further investigation on the basis of the information generated during the discussion between the informants and the principal investigator. It was decided to contact the voters of three constituencies namely, Nilakkottai, Athur, and Dindigul. The sample is designed in such a fashion as to get voters of different geographical area, different caste groups and different economic strata. The study team consisted of the project staff and researchers of the Department of Political Science and Development Administration, Gandhigram Rural Institute, visited nine villages and contacted five hundred and twenty-five voters. When the study team visited the villages, the political leaders had started their second round of campaign. It was ensured that the political parties visited the villages. They have been asked questions pertinent to their rationale behind their voting, their role in the political process, their role in the political socialization process, their views about the issues in the general election, their expectations from the candidates, their past experience in the elections and their relationship with the representatives. Moreover, they have been explicitly asked about their faith in parliamentary democracy and their views about the performance of the political parties. The respondents have enthusiastically responded to the questions posed by the investigators more than the expectations. The respondents who have supplied adequate or more information about the performance of the political system, are considered as the participants of political development. The results are analysed in the following pages.

RESULTS AND DISCUSSION

Democratic Commitment

Winning independence is the first step in the nation building process. Secondly the state machinery has to initiate steps to augment representative institutions. It involves creating representative institutions and conducting periodical elections. By doing so continuously people's commitment towards democracy could be strengthened. So far the people had seen twelve general elections. In the whole process they got information about election, representation legislature, executive, and governmental performance. To what extent the five decades of experience shaped the opinion of the people about the democratic form of government. For any political act, commitment, faith and loyalty of the people towards the political system are *sine quo non.* It is felt that the people could be asked specifically whether they have faith or commitment towards the democratic political process. The table given below gives the details of the response of the respondents.

Table 2.1 : Voters Faith in Democracy.

S. No.	*Category*	*No. of Respondents*	*%*
1.	Faith in Democracy	403	77
2.	No faith in Democracy	106	20
3.	No response	16	3
	Total	**525**	**100**

Source : Computed.

The rural people who have been interviewed were poverty stricken and most of them have declared that they have not conversed with the functioning of the political system. However because of their experience in participation in democracy. It is an interesting observation that despite the weakness of our democracy, we are able to run our democratic institutions without any crack is the overwhelming faith of the people in democracy and parliamentary institutions. But nearly 20 per cent of the people expressed their total dissatisfaction over the functioning of the democratic political system. They replied that they have lost faith in democracy. In the fifty-five years neither the political parties nor the government have done anything substantial to solve the problems of the people. Day by day they have been acquiring more powers to make themselves as demons. They have expressed that they have a fear whether the political parties are the stumbling block for the people's progress. It we witness any development in the society, it is despite our corrupt politicians and corrupt bureaucracy. This is their considered opinion.

Participation

Political participation is always linked with the development of a polity. Participation may differ from group to group depending on the socio-economic status of the people. However political participation is the result of political mobilization. The changes that occur in the attitude of the people due to modernization, technology and communication revolution, directly affect the political process of the nation by the participation of the people.

These changes provide the motivation and resources for political development on the part of individuals; they became aware of politics, learn norms of political participation of citizenry and develop the cognitive skills needed for political activity. In addition to these changes in the social situation of individuals and in their psychological predispositions towards political involvement, political institutions affect the political involvement of citizens.[15] Against this background, the people were asked about their previous political participation and their determination for participation.

Here the commitment of the people towards democracy and participation are analysed. Questions relating to their participation have been asked and the responses are given below :

Table 2.2 : Participation in the Previous Election.

S. No.	*Category*	*No. of Respondents*	*%*
1.	Participated	439	84.0
2.	Not Participated	82	15.3
3.	No response	4	0.7
	Total	**525**	**100.0**

Source : Computed.

Table 2.3 : Determination to Participate in the Election.

S. No.	*Category*	*No. of Respondents*	*%*
1.	Decided to participate	484	92.10
2.	Not yet decided	22	4.19
3.	No response	19	3:62
	Total	**525**	**100.00**

Source : Computed.

Table 2.4 : Determination to Vote for a Party.

S. No.	*Category*	*No. of Respondents*	*%*
1.	Decided to vote for a party	477	90.86
2.	Not yet decided	41	7.81
3.	No response	7	1.33
	Total	**525**	**100.00**

Source : Computed.

Mere expression of commitment towards does not help the system grow unless the faith is translated into action. Actions of the people in the political process of the country are of many types. Actions should be positive, continuous and stable. In this context, a battery of three questions have been asked. Have you casted your vote in the previous election? Are you going to caste you vote in the present election? Have you decided the candidate to whom you have to vote? For all the three questions, the respondents replied clearly. Nearly 84 per cent of them participated in the previous election and 92 per cent of them decided to participate in the present election and 90 per cent of them decided even the political party to which they have to vote. Thus the indications are positive in nature.

Some demographic factors do influence the political participation of the people. The factors such as education, income and occupational status have their own impact on the political activity of the people. Herein this aspect has not been seriously analysed.

Cognitive Orientation of the People

It is all the more important to indicate the rationale behind their participation. The participation may be due to compulsion or fun or any other reason. But for a healthier democracy, participation of the people in the electoral process should be on the basis of an overall understanding about the functioning of the political institutions.

Against this background, the voters' cognitive aspect has been studied. Primarily to test their cognition, they were asked about the candidates who are contesting in the election. Voters' reactions are given below:

Table 2. 5 : Awareness of the Voters about their Candidates.

S. No.	*Category*	*No. of Respondents*	*%*
1.	Know the name of the candidates	409	77.9
2.	Do not know the name	812	11.6
3.	No response	55	10.5
	Total	**525**	**100.0**

Source : Computed.

The above table shows the trend of the voters response towards the question. Nearly 78 per cent of the voters clearly know the names of the candidates contesting in the election. 12 per cent of them do not know the names of the candidates. Around 11 per cent of the voters have no interest at all. It shows the political apathy of the people. It is a general impression that the rural voters even without knowing the candidate, by seeing the symbol they are casting their votes. But it is disproved in this study. Voters are clearly knowing the names of the candidates and their background. It is a positive sign for political development. Another leading question which falls well within the framework of the cognition is whether the voters cast their votes purely by judging the merit of the candidates or the party. The below given table explains the response of the voters :

Table 2.6 : Voters preference to Party and Candidate.

S. No.	*Category*	*No. of Respondents*	*%*
1.	Preference to Candidate	134	25.5
2.	Preference to the Party	338	64.3
3.	Both	27	5.2
4.	No response	26	4.9
	Total	**525**	**100.0**

Source : Computed.

In a country where parochial and subject political culture predominantly prevalent, one may not expect the voters to prefer the choice of a candidate. It is obvious from the functioning of our political system, the party established its grip over the mass for all political activities. Purely the political system is oriented towards party. Against this background 25 per cent of the voters decide their vote on the merit of the candidates rather than the party. 64 per cent of the people expressed that they decide their votes on seeing of the symbol of the parties. It is not an irrational decision of the voters. Because knowing fully well that the political parties are the powerful instruments to articulate the people's grievances rather than the individual members. As individuals representatives cannot make any impact in the decision-making bodies. These preferences are positive factors for the representative institutions.

Evaluative Orientation of the People

After considering the cognitive orientation of the people, it is logical to analyse the evaluative orientation of the people. How voters evaluate the performance of the system? i.e., Government, political parties and the politicians. To analyse the evaluative aspect of voters preference, a chain of questions have been posed to the voters on various aspects. First, the voters have been asked whether the political parties have really shown any real interest in solving the problems of the people. The table given below depicts the response of the voters.

Table 2.7 : Peoples idea about the Political Parties Role in solving the Problems of the People.

S. No.	*Category*	*No. of Respondents*	*%*
1.	Political parties are taking efforts	373	71.1
2.	Political parties are not taking efforts	120	22.8
3.	No response	32	06.1
	Total	**525**	**100.0**

Source : Computed.

It is interesting to note that 71 per cent of the respondents replied that political parties are taking earnest efforts to solve the problems of the people. In the conversation some of them explained in details the way in which the party in power is taking steps to solve the problems by citing the policies and programmes of the government. Equally they cited certain events by which the opposition parties saved people from the draconian policies of the government. Generally government is involved in allocating values to various segments of the society. This is a continuous process. One group may get substantial benefits from the allocation of the government. The other group may not get the same amount as the other one. Here the group which is affected would view the government as anti-people. It is very difficult to get a unanimous opinion of the people about the political performance of the parties. But the respondents highlighted and appreciated both the ruling party and opposition parties for their services to the people. In a way it shows the balanced evaluation of the people about the role of political parties. Thus they posted strong arguments in favour of political parties. While talking about political parties many rural voters subtly remarked that the political parties are the manifestations of the aspirations of the common man. This argument corroborates with the people's preference to the political parties rather than candidates. No doubt, political parties are the change agents. Political parties are giving impetus to the upward mobility of the mass. On many occasions attitude and behaviour of the people could be changed by the constant and continuous interaction of political parties with the masses.

When the voters are very clear about the positive role of the political parties, investigator is tempted to move further to analyse an important factor which is deciding the victory of the candidate and party in the election. Though it is a very difficult question even to the researcher, it is being asked to know the opinion of the people. They artibuted several reasons or a combination of reasons. One important point is that the respondents are able to decide or analyse the factors responsible for the electoral victory. It may be incorrect or correct, the people level of understanding about polity has gone up. Table 2.8 depicts the picture of the response of the respondents.

Table 2.8 : Determining Factors in the Election Victory.

S. No.	*Category*	*No. of Respondents*	*%*
1.	Issues Projected	228	43.43
2.	No response	297	56.57
	Total	**525**	**100.00**

Source: Computed.

It is inferred from the above table that 43 per cent of the voters highlighted several issues that are going to decide the fate of the political parties. The issues ranging from charisma of the leader to corrupt practices of the politicians. The issues highlighted by the people are to some extent the issues brought before the people by the propaganda machinery during the electioneering. In one respect it is a positive sign for political development. Even the people in the remote villages are able to spell out the issues of the polity. But the rest 56.5 per cent of them have not cited the issues and in fact they are not able to indicate the issue. So the decision for voting is not on a rational basis after the evaluation of the promises of the political parties. When 56.5 per cent of the voters decided their option without considering the issues, the investigator is compelled to ask a strait question on what basis you are casting your vote? The responses are given below:

Table 2.9 : Basis of Voter's Choice.

S. No.	*Category*	*No. of Respondents*	*%*
1.	Political Party	193	38.5
2.	Ideology	124	24.7
3.	Party Leader	74	14.7
4.	Candidate	24	4.7
5.	Election Promises	21	4.2
6.	Others	89	13.2
	Total	**525**	**100.0**

Source: Computed.

Voters have more attachment towards the parties than on other aspects. About 39 per cent of the voters have expressed that their decision of voting is very much conditioned by the parties rather than the other issues. Likewise 24.7 per cent of the voters indicated that their decision is on the basis of the ideology of the party. 14.7 per cent of the voters said that their decision is very much influenced by the leaders. This break up gives a clue that the electoral victory is not judged by any single factor, it is a combination of factors. But of all the factors political party plays a major part.

While evaluating the performances and promises of the political parties and candidates, it is equally important to know that what expectation the people are casting their votes. When an individual is performing his role in the polity as a citizen, he has got every right to expect something from the system. This expectation is one of the aspects of political culture. Normally in third world countries people are oriented only in expecting the output of the government without considering the input of the government. If the people are giving more importance to input aspect of polity, the political culture of the country is a participatory one. If the people are always thinking about the output aspect of the political system, the political culture is subjective. In this context, to know the level of expecta-tion, a question has been asked as what do you expect from your representatives or your candidates after he/she became a representative. Table 2.10 gives the response of the voters.

Table 2.10 : Voters Expectation.

S. No.	*Category*	*No. of Respondents*	*%*
1.	Specific expectations	415	76.1
2.	No response	110	23.9
	Total	**525**	**100.0**

Source : Computed

76.1 per cent of the people have specifically stated that they have got greater expectation from the legislators as they are the policy makers and brokers between the people and the government. 23.9 per cent of the voters said that though they are casting their votes, they have no expectation from the legislator. The expectations are many. It ranges from individual to community, community to province, province to nation and nation to humanity. Most of their responses are centering around personal or individual demands and community demands.

It is logical on the part of the investigator to move from the area of the people's expectation to peoples experience. When the people expressed their expectation, it is obvious that the expectations are on the basis of the past experience. To what extent the representatives in the previous period fulfilled their expectations. To this question voters sharply reacted. The results are given below:

Table 2.11 : Voters Experience of Legislators Performance.

S. No.	*Category*	*No. of Respondents*	*%*
1.	Legislators fulfilled their promises	313	59.6
2.	Not fulfilled their promises	148	28.2
3.	No response	64	12.2
	Total	**525**	**100.0**

Source: Computed.

59.6 per cent of the respondents expressed that the legislators have tried their level best to meet the expectations of the people. Yet 28.2 per cent of the voters categorically said that the legislators have not fulfilled their promises and they work for their friends, relatives and clans. 12 per cent of the respondents are in total apathy.

Political Socialization

For evaluative orientation of the people towards the political system, one has to touch upon the political socialization of the citizenry. Political socialization process takes place in family, group and political party. Since family is playing a vital part in deciding political involvement of the people, what role the family plays in the political socialization and decision making is pertinent to political participation. Rural voters were asked as to what extent the family members discuss the political issues and events in the family among themselves during leisure hours. The responses are given below:

Table 2.12 : Discussion in the Family about Politics.

S. No.	*Category*	*No. of Respondents*	*%*
1.	Discuss political issues in the family	350	66.67
2.	No discussion	146	27.81
3.	No response	29	5.52
	Total	**525**	**100.0**

Source: Computed.

Majority of the members are in the joint family system. All the voters are from the rural areas. Yet they told the investigators that during the election time, they use to have intensive discussion about politics. The discussions were about the leaders of the political parties, credibility of the candidates and their social affiliations based on the information gathered by the members at the workplace, market and public meetings. Though all the members involved in the discussion, it is always a question whether all the members of the family got independence to take decision even though there is a possibility of changing the decision at the booth. In the Indian context the family decision for voting is a phenomenon in the electoral studies. Hence another question "who is taking decision with regard to voting?" has been asked. The responses are in the following table:

Table 2.13 : Decision-making in the Family for Voting.

S. No.	*Category*	*No. of Respondents*	*%*
1.	Individual decision	225	42.8
2.	Head of the family	227	52.3
3.	No response	25	4.9
	Total	**525**	**100.0**

Source: Computed.

Though majority of the members involved in the discussion about the polity in the family, only 42.8 per cent of the people exercised their choice in the voting. 52.3 per cent of the voters told that the direction would be given by the head of the family as to whom they have to vote. Thus the head of the family is a voter deciding the bunch of votes. Instead of voter, family is the entity in the voting behaviour of the society. It is still further confirmed by a question "will all your family members cast your votes for a single party?" Responses are given in table No. 2.14.

Table 2.14 : Family Members decision to vote for a Single Party.

S. No.	*Category*	*No. of Respondents*	*%*
1.	All members in a family vote for a single party	319	60.76
2.	Individuals vote differently	172	32.76
3.	No response	34	6.48
	Total	**525**	**100.0**

Source: Computed.

Under normal circumstance party members advice their family members to cast their vote in favour of his/her party. But sympathizers and neutral voters do not have such commitment as the member has. Hence they will not insist the family members to cast for a particular party. In the days of brokerage politics votes could be divided by way of giving money. While seeing the responses of the respondents, it is inferred that there is no division in the family with regard to decision for voting. 32.76 per cent of the voters replied that they would decide on their own.

Affective Orientation

Following the socialization process of the individuals in the family, affective orientation is taken up for analysis. The voters were asked about their political affiliation.

Table 2.15 : Party Affiliation.

S. No.	*Category*	*No. of Respondents*	*%*
1.	Affiliated with a political party	434	82.67
2.	No affiliation	84	16.00
3.	No response	7	1.33
	Total	**525**	**100.0**

Source: Computed.

82 per cent of the respondents indicated that they affiliated themselves with a political party. It does not mean that they are all

party members. Their sympathy is always with a particular political party. It is evident from the next two questions namely (a) Are you a sympathizer of a party? and (b) In what form have you participated in the election process? The answers are given in the following tables :

Table 2.16 : Party Sympathizer.

S. No.	*Category*	*No. of Respondents*	*%*
1.	Yes	383	72.95
2.	No	124	23.62
3.	No response	18	3.43
	Total	**525**	**100.0**

Source: Computed.

Table 2.17 : Mode of Participation.

S. No.	*Category*	*No. of Respondents*	*%*
1.	Casting vote	210	40.0
2.	Canvassing votes	81	15.4
3.	Attending party meeting	65	12.4
4.	Participating in the meeting	41	7.8
5.	Giving fund	17	3.2
6.	Participating in the procession	12	2.3
7.	Others	99	18.9
	Total	**525**	**100.0**

Source: Computed

72.9 per cent of the people expressed that they are sympathizers of political parties. While analyzing the mode of participation, it is clear that 40 per cent of the voters said that their participation is in voting. 15.4 per cent of the voters told that they actively involved in canvassing for the candidates. 12.4 per cent replied that they used to attend the political party meetings regularly. A few adopted other modes of participation in the political process. But the nature of participation of the voters varies from individual to individual.

Thus the aspect namely cognition of the voters, evaluative

capacity of the voters, participatory affiliation of the voters with the political party are described.

Analysis

From the above discussion one would infer that nearly 60 to 70 per cent of the voters have deep faith in the democratic process of the political system and the institutions and organizations involved in it. Their faith and commitment towards the party system and democratic governance are purely based on the cognition and evaluation of the people about the promises and performances of the organization and institutions legitimately identified with the governance of the society. People's identification with a party and inclination to uphold the governing body are the results of the rationalization process of the voters preferences. More so, it is the logical culmination of the political socialization[16] process that takes place in the family. Thus there is a reason to believe that the democratic values have been percolated into the mass even at the grassroots level. But at the same time nearly 30 to 40 per cent of the people have the political apathy which is not a good sign for the political development of the society. In the three constituencies, the survey team had a chat with a few voters for a long time. Here they are all designated as dialogue participants. Though they are hailing from the last rung of the society, their knowledge about the society, political system and the behaviour of the political leaders are highly valuable to the researchers to pursue research further. Some of their observations are brought forth here.

A good deal of chat with some of the rational voters reveals that voters of the villages have three different attitudes about the election and the parties. But one aspect is common to all the nine villages. Sometimes it may be common to all the villages in India. The total ignorance of the masses about the principles, objectives, goals, promise and manifestoes of the political parties is a common phenomena in the villages. Regarding all other aspects of electioneering, it is found that people exhibit variations in their thinking.

There are varieties of voters namely party oriented voters, group oriented voters, leaders oriented voters, interest oriented voters and candidate oriented voters. Of the voters the party oriented and leaders oriented groups have major voters strength. The voters have different perceptions about the parties, leaders and the governments.

Interesting observations are made while hearing from one Mr. Mathalaimuthu of Silukkuvarpatti. Though seemingly a poverty sticken man, his views reveal his myriad mindedness in politics, maturity and decisiveness in all aspects of polity and life. He was open, critical and suggestive in all his approaches towards the political problems. He changed his loyalty from the Congress to the AIADMK through the DMK and now in the DMK with the AIADMK sympathy. He cherished the memory of MGR, then Chief Minister of Tamil Nadu and he was educated in politics by MGR through his films. He lamented the plight of the Silukkuvarpatti people suffering from acute water shortage. He explained to the investigator that the lobby of the economically affluent section of the Pattiveeranpatti village played a major role in checking any move of the MLA to bring water to Silukkuvarpatti. Interestingly he is smart enough to give a link between the politicians and the moneyed class. He underlined the fact that the politicians are in the hands of the affluent section of the society. He is skeptical about the promises of the candidates. He said people in this village are fed up with this election. Party lobbies are here and they will work for their party at the eleventh hour. He further observed that AIADMK votes are silent votes. It could be known only in the ballot box. DMK votes are vociferous votes known in the street itself. He concluded that whether it is DMK or AIADMK or Congress I, the people are the pawns in the political chess board which could be used for the advantages of the advantaged and privileged group and this behaviour would continue as long as the people are ignorant and illiterate. Many more have been contacted in this village and all upheld the propositions of Mathalaimuthu. An interesting observation was made by a few voters about the mood of the people when they go to the booth to cast their votes. Everybody will go to the booth not with a sense of electing their representative, but they go to the place as if they go to the temple for a festival and beyond that to them it has no sanctity.

When the team visited the villages, people in village narrated a story of their practice in participating in the election. Near about thirty years they had a practice of taking decision in the village committee as to whom they had to vote? They have given up this practice for the past two general elections as the youth protested against this type of group decisions. Likewise behaviour of the voters vary from place to place. However the substantial number of voters evinced keen interest in political participation. In the course of conversation between the principal investigator and the development participant many new points have been developed for further investigation.[17]

Conclusion

It is beyond about that the people in the rural areas have firm faith in democracy and political parties. They do take active interest in the political process of the nation. Nearly 60 to 70 per cent of the people have deep commitment towards the democratic political institutions. With concern and expectation, they approach the government, political parties for all their problems. It is in the hands of the political parties to handle the people. If the parties continue to betray the people, the people would betray the democratic system. Nearly from 25 per cent to 30 per cent of the voters are having political apathy. 70 per cent of the people are deeply involved in the political system either covertly or overtly. It is obvious from the answers of the respondents that their commitment and involvement in the political system is positive in nature. Their cognitive, affective and evaluative orientations indicate that they are in the participative political culture. This is against the existing notion that Indian Political Culture is a mixture of parochial and subjective political culture. The incongruence between the existing notion and the reality is to be explained in terms of the nature and intensity of the people's commitment and involvement in the political system. This needs further validation and interpretation.

NOTES

1. Lucian W. Pye, Aspects of Politcal Development, New Delhi, Amerind Publishing Co., Panchayat . Ltd., 1966.
2. Ramashray Roy, "Electoral Politics" in ICSSR, *Survey of Research in Political Science: Political Process*, Vol. II, New Delhi: Allied Publishers Private Limited, 1981, pp.163-180.
3. V.M. Sirsikar, *Political Behaviour in India,* Bombay: Menakatalas, 1965.
4. Ramashray Roy, op. cit., pp.165-166.
5. Periodically Election Commission has brought out publication which provides data of the results and the votes secured by the parties and the candidates.
6. C. Parvathamma, "Election and Traditional Leadership in Mysore Village", *Economic and Political Weekly*, 17, (1C & 11) 7 and 14, March 1964; Rajni Kothari and Tarun Sheth, "Extent and Limits of Community Voting: The case of Baroda East" in Centre for the Study on Developing Societies, *Party System and Election Studies*, Occasional Papers 1, New Delhi: Allied Publishers, 1967.
7. Ramashray Roy, "Selection of Congress Candidates" *Economic and Political Weekly*, 1 (2) 31 Dec., 1966; Surinder Suri, "Campaign", *Seminar* 34 (June, 1962); B.B. Patil, "Campaign Strategy and Voting Behaviour", *Economic and Political Weekly*, 3 (1 & 2) Jan, 1968.
8. Surinder Suri, "Towards a Theory of Indian Politics", *The Economic Weekly* 14 (48) 1 Dec., 1962, Iqbal Narain and M.Lal, "Election Politics in India: Notes Towards and Empirical Theory", *Asian Survey*, 9 (3) March 1969.
9. Rajasthan University has done a commendable work in this area.
10. Samuel J. Eldersveld, "Theory and Method in Voting Behaviour Research", in Heinz Eulau, Samuel J. Eldersveld and Morris Janowitze, (eds.) *Political Behaviour: A Reader in Theory and Research*, New Delhi: Amerind Publishing Co. Pvt. Ltd., 1956, pp. 267-307.
11. Graham Wallas, "Human Nature in Politics" in Heinz Eulau, Samuel, J. Eldersveld and Morris Janowitz (eds) *Political Behaviour: A Reader in Theory and Research*, New Delhi: Amerind Publishing Co. Pvt. Ltd., 1972, p. 9.
12. Julian L.Woodward and Elmo Roper, "Political Activity of American Citizens" in Heinz Eulau et. Al (eds) *Political Behaviour: A Reader in Theory and Research*, New Delhi: Amerind Publishing Co. Pvt. Ltd., 1972, p.133.
13. Robert E.Agger and Vincent Ostrom, "Political Participation in a Small Community" in Heinz Eulau et. al. (eds) op. cit., p.138.
14. Political culture and political participation have been extensively studied. Pioneering works are: Wie, Normai and Sidney Verba, "Political Participation" in *Handbook of Political Science* (eds.) Fred Greenstein and Nelson Polsby, New York: Addision-Wesley, 1975; Gabriel A.Almond and Sidney Verba, *The Civic Culture*, Princeton: Princeton University Press, 1963; Sidney Verba, Normal H.Nie, Jac on Kim, *Participation and Political Equality*, Cambridge: Cambridge University Press, 1978.

15. David E.Apter, *Choice and the Politics of Allocation A Developmental Theory*, New Heaven, Conn: Yale University Press, 1971.
16. Dennis Kavonaogh, *Political Culture*, London: Macmillan, 1972, pp. 28-36.
17. Regarding the opinion of the individuals about the development, one can refer to an excellent work Ramashray Roy and R.K. Srivastava, *Dialogues on Development: The Individual Society and Political Order,* New Delhi: Sage, 1986.

BIBLIOGRAPHY

Almond A. Gabriel and Sidney Verba, *The Civic Culture,* Princetion : Princetion University Press, 1963.

Apter E. David, *Choice and the Politics of Allocation. A Developmental Theory,* New Heaven, Conn : Yale University Press, 1971.

Eulau Heinz, Samuel J. Eldersveld and Morris Janowitze, (eds) *Political Behaviour : A Reader in Theory and Research,* New Delhi : Amerind Publishing Co. Pvt. Ltd., 1956.

Greenstein Fred and Nelson Polsby (eds), *Handbook of Political Science,* New York : Addision-Wesley, 1975.

Kavonaogh Dennis, *Political Culture,* London : Macmillian, 1972.

Kothari Rajni and Tarun Sheth, Extent and Limits of Community Voting : The Case of Baroda East" in *Centre for the Study on Developing Societies, Party System and Election Studies,* Occasional Paper 1, New Delhi : Allied Publishers, 1967.

Narain Iqbal and M. Lal, "Election Politics in India : Notes Towards and Empirical Theory", *Asian Survey,* 9(3) March 1969.

Paravathamma C., "Election and Traditional Leadership in Mysore Village," *Economic and Political Weekly,* 17, (IC & 11) 7 and 14, March 1964.

Patil, B.B., "Compaign Strategy and Voting Behaviour", *Economic and Political Weekly,* 3(1 & 2) January 1968.

Pye W. Lucian, *Aspects of Political Development,* New Delhi, Amerind Publishing Co. Pvt. Ltd., 1966.

Roy Ramashray and R.K. Srivastava, *Dialogues on Development : The Individual Society and Political Order,* New Delhi : Sage, 1986.

Roy Ramashray, "Electoral Politics" in ICSSR, *Survey of Research in Political Science : Political Process,* Vol. II, New Delhi : Allied Publishers Private Limited, 1981.

Roy Ramashray, "Selection of Congress Candidates", *Economic and Political Weekly,* 1(2) December., 1966.

Sirsikar V.M., *Political Behaviour in India,* Bombay : Menakatalas, 1965.

Suri Surinder, "Campaign", *Seminar* 34, June, 1962.

Suri Surinder, "Towards a Theory of Indian Politics," *The Economic Weekly* 14 (48) 1 December, 1962.

Verba Sidney, Normal H. Nie, Jac on Kim, *Participation and Political Equality,* Combridge : Combridge University Press, 1978.

INDEX